TALES from the TYPEWRITER SHOP

Dennis Everest

SEDAN CHAIR

PUBLISHING

LONDON

Special Edition
Published 2010 by
SEDAN CHAIR PUBLISHING CO.,
24 St.Dunstan's Hill,
Cheam,
Surrey.
ENGLAND

ISBN 978-0-9551662-9-7

British Library Cataloguing
Publication Data: a Catalogue
of this book is availiable
from the British Library.

Printed in England

CONTENTS

TALES from the TYPEWRITER SHOP

INTRODUCTION

Life in the Typewriter Shop is a true tale of a husband and wife team working together for 35 years and dealing with over a quarter of a Million people and their Writing Machines. A chance purchase of one broken typewriter 35 years ago has now led to their dealing with over one hundred thousand. Their exotic tales of travel around the World are highly illustrated as they search for Export markets to expand their business and at the same time travelling for pleasure and adventure to countries including Kenya, Zimbabwe, Barbados, Greenland, Egypt, Nubia, Canada, Jordan and the USA, often flying at twice the speed of sound on board Concorde. Whilst back in the shop they recall 50 strange tales of some of their difficult, more unusual, sometimes bizarre customers that they meet.

Chapter 1
THE TYPEWRITER SHOP
HOW IT ALL STARTED

One day a well known Author called into the shop to collect his small Olivetti manual portable typewriter, one that we had repaired and serviced.

He said, I am so pleased to have this back, I have had it for years and have written ten books on it, all published by John Murray of London.

Suddenly, he said to me." Look, you know all about these writing machines that thousands of people like me earn our living on. We have used them all our lives, and yet we know little about them."

He went on to say, "you could do several books on the subject," you could write for us the history of the writing machine, just look at the huge range that you have on show. You could even write about your shop, and especially your travels I am sure there must be a good tale there as well.

I am an engineer, I can't write I replied, to which he responded; That does not matter; just write as you would talk to us, someone else can correct the grammar.

I was a bit surprised by his comments, but in the back of my mind I was thinking, what a good idea, after all I had been a serious collector of writing machines for many years and had over a 100 dating from the early days of 1880 to the present day. Also, to recall and tell the Tales of the Shop and our Travels, that would be an interesting task for me to do. There are few in the world who can beat the excitement of our business come pleasure world travel adventures.

And so further encouraged and urged on, I began, this is the start of (Book 1). Tales from the Typewriter Shop.

******

This is a true tale of Rags to Riches and Fame and Fortune in a modest way. It was about 1970 or so, when a good friend of mine who was working as a Purchasing Manager for a large Bank, said to me: "I know you like inventing things in your workshop and I was wondering whether you would like to purchase from my bank some redundant dictation machines that are about to be replaced. I thought you might like them to take apart for the nuts and bolts and other bits and pieces in the machines." He went on to say that they were working but for company tax efficiency, they were renewed every four years.

As life at that time was not easy and I was always looking

for new ideas to improve my hard-up lot, my immediate reply was: "Thank you Bob, I will be very pleased to take up your offer." I therefore became the proud owner of 20 Grundig dictation machines along with their microphones and headsets, I agreed to pay at the end of the month the asking price which was £2 each and so for £40 I had this huge pile of old machines filling up my garden workshop.

What to do with them now I thought, bearing in mind that £40 was about two weeks wages for me in those days and with two young children, a wife and a large mortgage, I was spending money I could ill afford and which I barely had, in fact did not have. What I did have was only until the end of the month to raise the £40. So thinking hard I worked out what I thought was a good idea, number one we could sell the baby's cot and she could sleep in the that empty bottom drawer in the three-drawer bedroom cabinet, and number two perhaps the wife's engagement ring, (she doesn't need that now) it could go as well.

However, before I was mistreated, fate and a kind dad came to our aid, my father had won just over £50 on the football pools and he helped out by giving us £20, the other £20 I just about managed to scrape together, which meant the ring and the baby's bed were saved. I still reckon she would have liked it in that bottom drawer.

Not knowing anything about these strange things I had bought. I wondered what could be done with this number of machines. I decided to take stock of what was to be seen. I looked at the sales market for new and reconditioned machines of this nature and was surprised to find that I had in my possession, machines that I could strip down, recondition so they looked and worked like new, and then sell on to a new grateful owner for ten times the price I had paid. This seemed to me to be a pretty good idea, so my thoughts naturally were to look out for more deals of this kind. More deals came along, not as regularly as I would have liked, but now and again a batch of machines would turn up.

Some months later this same friend offered me a scrap manual typewriter that his company was disposing of. He said "It is an Adler manual only three years old but the bank's typewriter suppliers said it is scrap, broken beyond repair. They offered the bank £10 in part exchange against the purchase of a new machine. I thought of you and your workshop so if you want it for the same price, you can have it. I will do the bank's paperwork and bring it home to you.

My thoughts were racing, a Typewriter I knew what they were but I had never touched one, so do I really want one, least of all a scrap one and a Tenner that's half a weeks wages, but something in me said take a chance, so my reply was "Thanks very much Bob, I will look forward to that."

I had never touched a typewriter let alone owned one, this should be great I thought, I was feeling quite excited. I sensed there was to be something else from this deal, something apart from a £10 scrap machine and I was right, this one broken typewriter was to lead us to dealing with over one hundred thousand and was to completely change our way of life. It introduced us to a world of Supersonic Travel, and the EVEREST TYPEWRITER Company was about to be born.

I purchased the typewriter which was a 15" Adler 390. and paid the asking price of £10 and after I had repaired it in my workshop, I advertised it and sold it straight away to a very excited man who could see it was a bargain for £120. Apparently the new price for one of these machines was over £300. The repair was not a standard typewriter mechanic's type of repair, it was more of a mechanical engineer's job. In fact it was right up my street. I had served a six year engineering apprenticeship in the aircraft industry followed by two years in the Royal Air Force working on aircraft maintenance. I also had at that time, a further twelve years experience working in industry and research laboratories.

I was highly skilled and technically qualified so repairing this typewriter was not a problem to me. I now realised, with my experience and mechanical skills, I could easily create a business in rebuilding and reconditioning Typewriters and Dictation Machines and so it was to be.

About 1972, I opened a shop in "Railway Approach", a British Rail premises. The British Rail's Property Letting Agent said they required £400 a year rent. I looked at the property, the floor and walls were soaking wet, in a deplorable condition and consisted of one main room with an adjacent room with a leaking toilet. I offered them £80 a year stating-that was all it was worth. Their reply came back that they accepted my offer. It was obvious they were only too pleased to get somebody in to sort out the bad state, so a deal was done. EVEREST TYPEWRITERS CO now had a base to work from and we were about to become an established Retail Shop.

A couple of years after starting my first shop in Railway Approach, I opened up a second High Street shop which is situated at traffic lights along side a busy main approach road heading into London. It has four lanes (2 each way) carrying traffic at the rate of about one car a second, well over 50,000 a day, that's around 15,000,000 (15 million) vehicles a year whose drivers and passengers see us and our Illuminated shop sign as they pass by or stop at the nearby traffic lights.

Being the first shop means it is a good spot to get noticed. It is located at the start of a block of some ten other various types of shops, next door to us is a Car showroom followed by a Kebab shop, an Indian takeaway, a Ladies hairdressers, a Betting shop, another Car showroom, an all day breakfast Cafe, and then the Gander a large Pub, and in a flat above one of the shops is a "Knocking" shop crewed by a number of ladies who always look smart and seem happy with their lot .

This is a busy parade full of choices that could strain or tempt most men one way or another, starting with all the expensive fancy cars on show that maybe they could ill afford to buy, the tantalising smells of fast fancy food that if they bought in excess might further expand their girth, and the thought of those lovely beer pumps all lined up erect just waiting for an order for a pint to be pulled, followed by a call on the bookmaker for the excitement of a flutter or two risking their shirts on that sure thing, and there are all the fancy ladies relaxed and perfumed just waiting for their doorbell to be rung. With all these temptations to strain the thinking, there are some men who

might need the hand of God to help them to resist, well there is a small Church to cover that possibility as well, so all in all we are a pretty lively and interesting parade full of temptations and choices.

The Typewriter shop is also full of choices, the pictures taken in December 2008 shows part of a side wall displaying our range of Writing Machines. Top shelf are the Manual Portable Typewriters always wanted by millions of people that are fed up with too much technology. Next shelf is for people who like technology a range of Word Processors, with popular names such as Adler, Sharp, Brother, and Cannon all with near laser quality printing, and a disk drive system for storing information. This type of advanced machine is nearly as good as a computer for typed work and further more it does not have the dangers of the Internet which for some religious groups is a Godsend. Why? Because they believe the Devil is deep inside and controls the Internet, and so they ban the personal use of computers to their followers. Next shelf are office and home electronic typewriters with self-correction and memory features. Next shelf a range of office manual typewriters, Imperial, Olivetti, Adler, and Olympia. These machines are attractive to a number of people including authors who like the non-technical action that gives the tap tap and the ding of the carriage-return bell. An old saying was: (The hearing of the tap tap of an old trusty friend seems to reciprocate a bonding that encourages the flow of thought). And on the floor are customers repairs waiting for collection.

The other picture shows on the opposite wall a range of electronic portable typewriters, dictation machines and a row of antique typewriters, often needed as film and stage props or Museums and the growing band of collectors. We often have 100 different types of machine on our shelves, ranging from a 1880 Antique to the new machines of today. Just like the parade we are full of choices.

Our Typewriter shop being at the start of this parade has some advantages and some disadvantages.

It was a standard size (before extending) shop but single floor only. I laid it out with shelves all along two side walls, a window display and desks in the middle of the floor, these were for customers to try out machines, and a very small area for servicing and repairs at the back. We had not been open long, only four days, when we had our first of many to come, night-time telephone calls from the local Police asking us to come down to the shop straight away.

When I arrived at the shop some 15 minutes later, there was glass everywhere. I spoke to one of the policemen who said witnesses had seen a small van reverse into the plate-glass window and then drive off fast. Apparently one witness said it was a red van which turned out of our service road and went left. However, another witness said it was a white van which turned right. So, there you are. Whatever and whoever it was, was not discovered but I have always thought it to be a local competitor who resented me coming into the area. The window replacement men were magic. They turned out straight away, took measurements for the replacement glass then boarded up for the remainder of the night. Next morning at about 9 a.m. they were there with a van and glass which was one huge pane half an inch thick and measuring 14ft by 8ft. A quick lift and a heave-ho and the new window was in. A dash around with a broom and they were off. You would never have known it had happened. Inside however, it was a different story, thousands of glass splinters were everywhere. What a way to start a business!

Like life everywhere, it pays to get to know the locals, not the Pubs, the people. There is always one who knows what is what. In this case it was old Sid. One day he asked me if it was damp around the back of the shop. Bearing in mind the back of the shop was a workshop area which was an old wooden type of construction, pretty old and knackered. I said to him that I did not think so. But Sid chuckled and said that it should be, because when the nearby Pub closed after lunch times the local lads go in to the betting shop next door for an hour or two and then when nature demands they dash round the back of our shop for a jimmy riddle and they had been doing this for as long as he could remember which was over 25 years. "Well Sid," I said, "I think it's time for me to sort this out, a change of practice is needed here."

Before doing a major building job, I erected some corrugated-steel sheeting around the side walls of the wooden building but this still did not deter the jimmy riddlers from using it. I tried shouting at them but this had little effect apart from one chap who staggered up to me and handed me his business card and apologised. He then staggered back to the betting shop. Others said; "OK, sorry mate." There was one extremely tough looking gentleman who turned round at my call and replied with a short expletive which suggested I should go off somewhere. It was about this time that I decided that pursuing this line of action might not be a good idea. It would not be too long before I ended up with a black eye and probably a punch on the nose for good luck, after all I was attempting to change a well-established routine.

I eventually decided to replace the old wooden structure with a proper brick building plus adding a whole new second floor to complete the job, and double the shop area and our working space. This finally solved the problem and gradually the long, old established habit of the jimmy riddlers faded away.

Selling anything to anybody always has its difficulties but selling complicated machines to people who have to develop considerable skills to operate them, is at best very difficult and hard work and sometimes, at least, nigh on impossible. Being successful in selling machines such as typewriters, word processors, and computers is fraught with difficulty. Firstly one has to equip the showroom with a good range of stock. For example, the range of writing machines we display on our shelves, amount to fourteen different versions of type and make, both new and reconditioned but it does not stop there because there are numerous makes all of which have their followers in the general public. To name a few companies there are Adler, Imperial, Olympia, Olivetti, IBM, these are probably the longest-standing manufacturers and some are still around and producing machines after many, many years. Other more recent makes are Smith Corona, Sharp, Brother, International, Silver Reed and Panasonic and there are many others such as Nakajima which has been our favourite and most reliable make for many years, and still is. We have sold many thousands of Nakajima machines. Servicing is most important as machines are no good if they are not functioning properly and therefore, routine

A part of our shop display (December 2007). The writing machines seen on the top shelf are Manual Portable Typewriters. The next shelves are Word Processors - the makes are Adler, Sharp, Brother and Canon. Next shelf are office daisywheel memory typewriters. the next shelves are manual office typewriters, Imperial, Olivette, Adler, Olympia. On the floor are customer's repairs awaiting collection.

We normally have up to 100 different types of typewriters available.
This picture shows top shelf 100's of various ribbons. Next two
shelves various Electronic Typewriters. Lower shelf a few of our
Antique Typewriters.these are often purchased by collectors, also the
Theatre and Film industry and Museums.

servicing is a good preventer of more serious breakdown, but breakdown they do from time to time. So it is necessary for us to carry in stock parts for machines which have a known regular fault problem. We also keep in our stores a range of old machines to dismantle for parts that are no longer available from the manufacturers. It would not be unusual for our storeroom to have 50 or more of these old machines which we can cannibalise.

The next chapter shows us two major events that have changed our way of writing. They effected everyone, but few know about it.

Chapter 2 shows us how.

Chapter 2
CHANGES TO THE WORLDS
WAY OF WRITING

From early times man has needed to record events. Chinese writers used fine brushes, Egyptians used pens made from reeds, Romans used metal rod pens, Europeans used geese and swan feathers (quills) sharpened into pen nib shapes. These quills lost their popularity after 1830 and the invention of the disposable split end metal pen nib. From those days on, until the present day, only two major changes have taken place to effect the (way we all write).

First was the gradual change from handwriting with a quill or a dip pen, to writing with a mechanical device, known worldwide as the Typewriter, this was the long awaited answer to get away from the bad illegible handwriting that was all to common and to achieve print quality (clear writing) from a machine that would sit on a desk.

Second, the greatest change to the modern history of our world's way of writing was the invention of the electronic silicon chip and the printed circuit boards, these and many other new linked inventions brought about a rapid change of pace in the writing machine design and technology.

These two major events have led to the development of the electronic typewriters, wordprocessors, and computers.

The new modern machines as they took over from the older styled ones, were to change forever, the world's way of writing!

These inventions suddenly created a massive high pressure sales drive, that came from all the major writing machine manufactures as they aimed at getting their new modern miracles into all our places of work.

Offices, schools and homes, were targeted so successfully that it resulted in replacing some 10 million manual office typewriters that became unwanted, redundant, and surplus to requirements throughout the UK alone. These no-longer wanted redundant machines were not consigned to the scrap-metal yard as one would expect, far from it, they became sought after and very valuable objects.

Huge numbers of trader's from the world's poorer countries seized their chance and would come here in their droves to eagerly buy up this massive number of redundant machines, for they knew, once they were back at home with their haul, there were fortunes to be made. It would be a quick sell up, a turnaround, and they would be back here eagerly seeking for more.

THE WORKINGS OF A MODERN WRITING MACHINE

The green printed circuit board is showing its network of soldered joints and circuitry. This one is also showing faults caused by liquid being spilt into the keyboard.

The brown board is the top side showing a number of silicon chips - the black rectangular shapes - and many other electronic components. This is a main board from a modern writing machine.

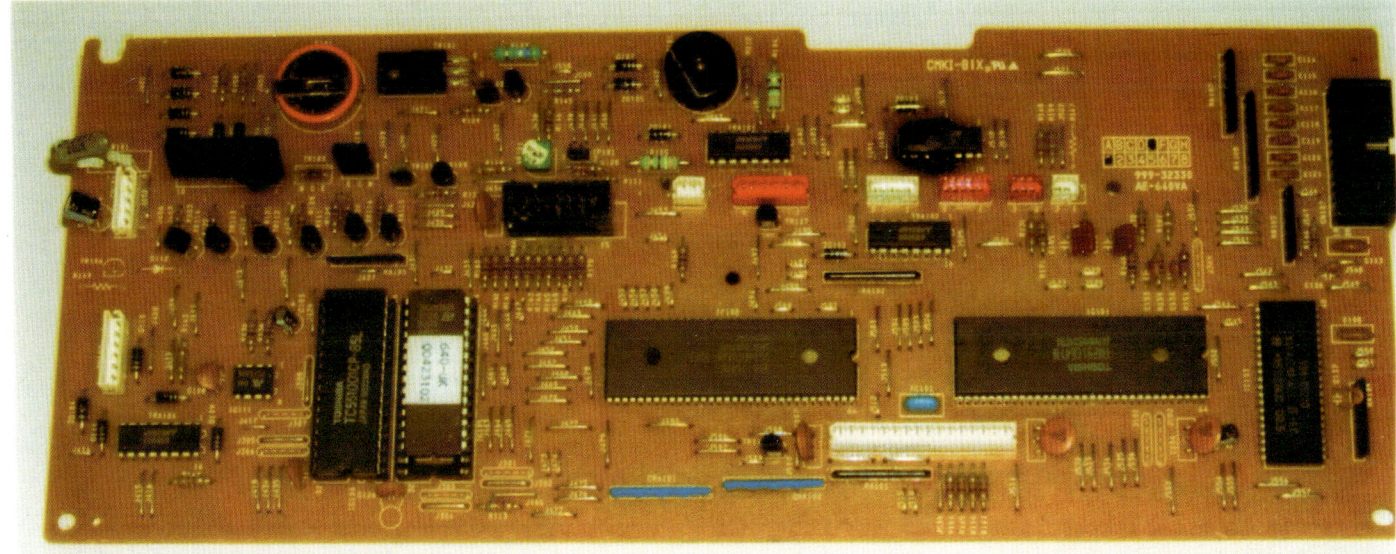

This flow of Third World buyers had all the ingredients similar to the old-days of the Wild West Gold Rush, this time the gold they were panning for was our country's 10 million surplus to requirements manual office typewriters. These machines were as good as gold nuggets once they had them back in their home country.

The time had come for many Third World countries to move there writing skills forward. They were hungry to train their people to enter in their masses, this mechanical way of writing. Economically, our unwanted old style now surplus writing machines that had become available in such large numbers, were now, with much excitement, within their reach.

To become a larger part of this massive project involving the sale and shipment of these redundant machines, we decided to make ourselves known to these foreign buyers. We would advertise in the press and make our shop known to the trade mission departments in various foreign Embassies. We used all of our efforts in every way we could to play as big a part as possible in the sales of our country's 10 million redundant machines. (Worldwide many 100's of millions of these old style writing machines were on the move).

This became a process that would last for one and a half decades.

Fired up and full of energy we also decided to travel abroad to search for more traders and sales contacts in the very heart of some of these overseas countries. As well as waiting for foreign buyers to find us, we would go and try to find them, to search them out. This added to the excitement of our part played in this massive, but little known about, world wide machine migration which we knew would not last for ever. Like the old style Gold Rush it was to be very exciting and rewarding until the source runs out.

In the following chapters, we illustrate and detail some of our exhilarating, often mind blowing, foreign travel, as we explore a number of countries around the world that are English Qwerty keyboard users.

In these countries there would be good possibilities for us to meet the right people to export some of these redundant manual machines to.

The changes to the world's writing machines had given us a world market to travel to, as such we travelled to many exotic places, from the heat of Africa to the cold of the Arctic, with the added flair of frequently flying supersonic on Concorde.

We travelled for business and we would always make it a leisure and adventure trip as well.

EVEREST RECONDITIONED TYPEWRITERS

TOP LEFT: An order for 50 manual typewriters for a school in Ghana.

TOP RIGHT: An order in 1995 for 60 machines for a college in Kenya, including some of the massive early Electronic Typewriters.

BOTTOM CENTRE: Part of an order for 100 manual typewriters for villages in Somalia.

Just like the old wild west "Gold Rush", buyers from the world's poorer nations flocked here in large numbers to eagerly buy up millions of our Country's unwanted typewriters. They knew that once they had taken their haul back to their homelands there were fortunes to be made.

Chapter 3
WORLDWIDE TRAVEL
AT LEISURE AND HUNTING FOR
EXPORT MARKETS

Writing Machines nowadays are in use all around the World, in every country, rich or poor. They come in various forms: there is the manual, electric, and electronic typewriters, the dedicated word processors and the range of computers, lap-tops, desk machines, and main-frame complexes.

As all ready explained, many of the poorest Third World countries had little money for such luxuries. However, with the coming in recent years of the modern computers, word-processor, and electronic typewriters, the availability of our country's now surplus older typewriters had become numerous. Ten Million of the older style manual and electric typewriters had now become available at a very cheap price, just what the poorer nations needed. It meant more and more colleges and training centres would now be set up to train typists in their millions just as we in the developed world have done so since 1880, the past 130 years or so.

The entrepreneurial businessmen and women from the African continent and of course, all other continents and needy countries around the world, looked eagerly to buying from the richer country's their unwanted machines.

They took to buying them in every way they could and in huge numbers.

Getting these typewriters from us to the middle of say Africa can be an expensive move. However, one way some of our overseas buyers would use to save on costs was to buy a large van then purchase a number of second-hand chest freezers, usually about six or eight, that would fit into the van. These freezers would then be filled with typewriters, the idea of all this putting one thing inside another, is to lower the shipping costs. The van would be driven, fully loaded, to the docks where it and its full load of contents would be taken aboard as one vehicle. It would then be shipped to its destination. On arrival, all the assembled buys together with the van, would be sold and then another flight booked to come back here to repeat the operation. Other more organized buyers would hire a ship's container which, for readers who are not sure what a ship's container is, it is a very large steel box with doors on the front. These containers vary in size. The ones our buyers used were about the size of a very large room. These could hold over 1,000 typewriters. These containers are used to transfer a wide variety of goods by ship securely all around the world.

As well as the overseas buyers that visit us, we are often called upon to supply typewriters to home-based exporting companies. When orders for typewriters had been taken by these companies they would come to us to fulfil their supply needs. It would usually be for our reconditioned manual typewriters. For example, one company supplying and fitting kitchens for the Ugandan Army came to me one day and explained that whilst working there, they had obtained an order for twenty, very long carriage, reconditioned manual typewriters. A carriage length of 28" was asked for. The idea in Africa was that the longer and bigger the carriage, the more value you had for your money. In this instance not realistic as 28" carriage typewriters were very rare. Eventually we settled on 18" carriage machines. These we had available and after refurbishment, the typewriters were sent on their way off to Uganda and a new life.

A number of my foreign orders came from a man who has become a good friend. He was running a company exporting anything anywhere. It could be flatbottom boats to the Nile Delta or bowler hats to Bolivia. Contact with me of course, was for typewriter orders. Being a practising Christian, he had contacts all over the world. He was able to contact fellow Christians in their vast numbers. For many years he would constantly come in with typewriter orders to fill, these going off to countries everywhere. It might be twenty machines to a school in Sierra Leone or several machines to a mission station in Mozambique or perhaps a single typewriter to a nun in Nigeria.

In order to enhance our own trading position in the export of these older redundant machines, we decided to make arrangements to travel abroad to search out and expand our Typing Machine Sales Markets.

Worldwide there are many countries using the English QWERTY keyboard. To contact their Business users and Trade buyers would mean a good deal of planning and high costs to get to them. However, I decided this we would try to do. We would travel to search for business and at the same time where possible, we would add pleasure and adventure to the trip. Our first exciting venture along these lines was to be off to the continent of Africa.

My foreign travels for the last 15 years or more have been dominated by my desire to get a good deal.

Having to constantly fight our typewriter supply companies representatives over the prices we pay for the machines we order from them, has sharpened my wits in such a way that I never expect to pay the asking price for almost anything anywhere. When it comes to holidays and travel, I have developed this cut price deal-making into a fine art. For the last 15 years or so, I have only taken foreign travel offers that were half price or an extra special price. I will explain. I buy my holidays like I buy my new typewriter stock, that is, the more you study and know about the people and companies your are dealing with, the more knowledge you have for recognising a good deal when you see it. My technique is that I have limited my travel choices to three high quality holiday companies. These three companies offer the finest means of travel, the finest venues, the finest guides, excellent food, hotels, tours and staff. Their complete itinerary is always exciting and excellent. However, they are to most peoples pockets, mine included, very expensive. My technique of learning and understanding the marketing manner of just a few companies allows me to study and know when a company will offer or accept a (Two for One) price deal. Even expensive holidays can look much more agreeable when they are half price!

Another thing is, when you study and know your chosen company's venue for the year, you will learn to know when a so called special offer is indeed a special offer. Sometimes they are just seasonal price adjustments, however some travel companies will do a one off really special experimental trip. They will hire a plane or a hotel or a large part of both, then they could try out and plan a potential new holiday package that they could add to a future year's brochure. Sometimes they even throw in Club Class seating on the aircraft or charter Concorde from British Airways.

Of course, when Concorde was flying, everything was beyond First Class. There is nothing finer than travelling on the edge of space, ten miles high, nearly 1400 miles an hour - that is a mile every 2½ seconds. Looking out of the window one sees the gentle curve of our planet. Touching the side panel of the aircraft one experiences a slight warmth caused by the speed and friction with the outside air and yet on the other side of that warm fuselage panel, the temperature is a freezing -50°c. The fine food served such as the lobster starter, the fillet steak dinners, the finest burgundy and vintage port wines, everything superb and for me it felt even better when I know I have only paid half the price of my fellow travellers, when I am on a special two for one deal.

Most good deals, special trips and so on, are often at short notice. One has to be well prepared for short notice travel. Not all people can arrange this, so for them there will be less opportunity but the chances though reduced, with careful planning can sometimes be possible. Another point about the real one' off special offers, is that they are usually holidays advertised in the weekend press. If the deal is really good, other people will also recognize the fact and all seats could sell out by the Monday morning. The really good special deals usually only need advertising once. With 2 for 1 deals some companies find that if they have vacant places left one or two weeks before departure then they will be only too pleased to fill those places. Your half price offer deal can be very welcome news to some travel companies. Simply put an empty seat is a total loss. A final tip is if you get a special deal, say a high discount or a 2 for 1 offer, whatever, it is a good idea not to go boasting to all the other travellers about your good fortune, be the gentleman or lady and keep your good news to yourself. That way you will prevent envy and you will keep the friends you make.

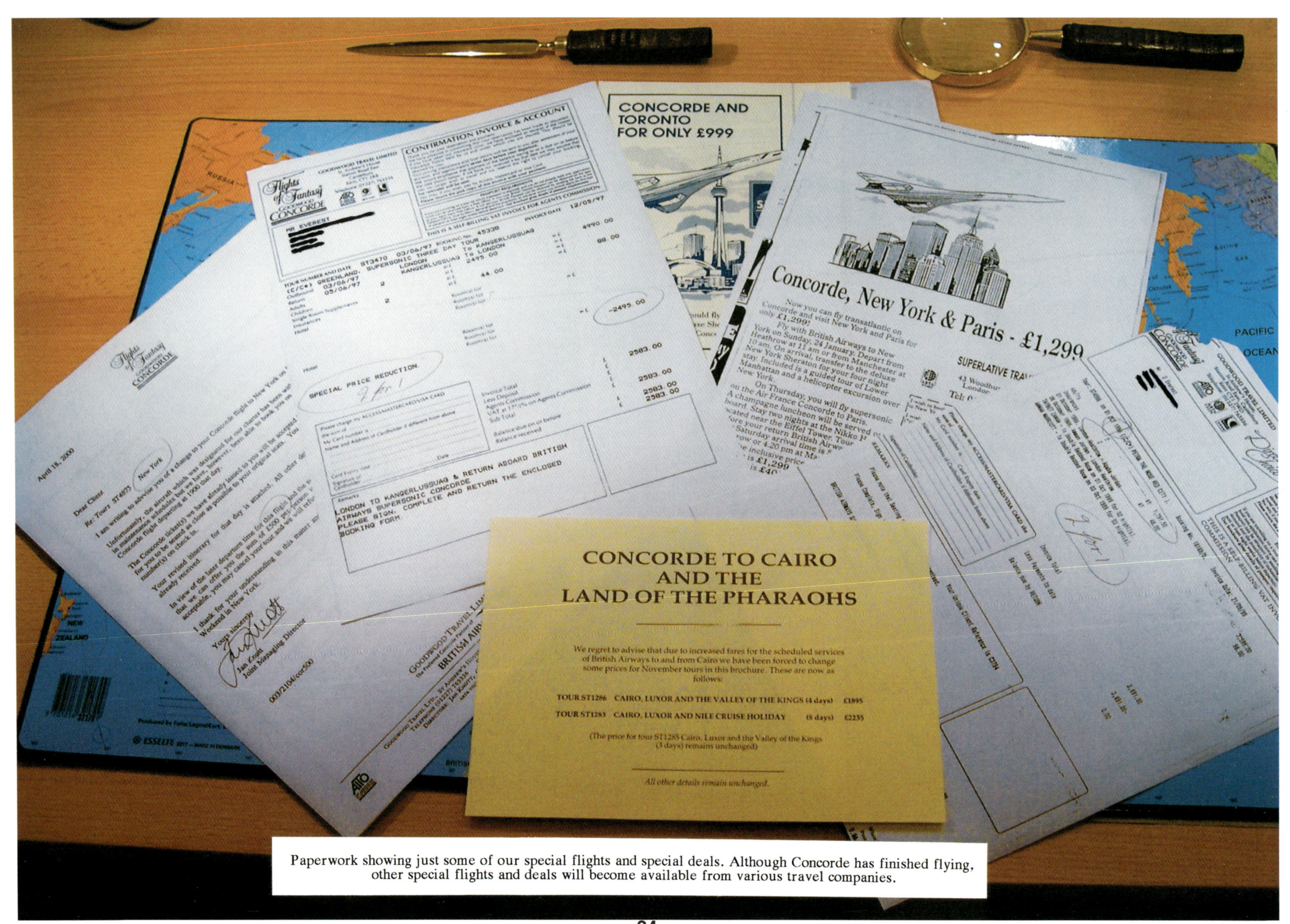

Paperwork showing just some of our special flights and special deals. Although Concorde has finished flying, other special flights and deals will become available from various travel companies.

These are some of the trips we have taken on two for one deals or extra special offers. Although Concorde is no long flying, other special deals will be available.

CONCORDE   BUSINESS CLASS   CLUB CLASS

<u>DESTINATION</u>

1)	KENYA - MOMBASSA	SPECIAL OFFER
2)	CANADA - TORONTO	CONCORDE - SPECIAL FLIGHT
3)	EGYPT - CAIRO	CONCORDE - SPECIAL FLIGHT
4)	EGYPT - LUXOR	CLUB CLASS
5)	JORDAN - AMMAN	CONCORDE - 2 for 1
6)	JORDAN - AQABA	CONCORDE - 2 for 1
7)	GREENLAND - KANGERLUSSUAQ	CONCORDE - 2 for 1
8)	USA - NEW YORK	CONCORDE - 2 for 1
9)	NEW YORK - PARIS	CONCORDE SPECIAL FLIGHT
10)	BARBADOS	BUSINESS CLASS SPECIAL
11)	ZIMBABWE	BUSINESS CLASS SPECIAL

When one is able to travel Concorde, Business or Club Class, not only do you benefit from better seating and spacing but you also benefit from the special airport lounges that are set aside for the high flyer. The lounges include a free bar, food and sometimes, computer rooms for the business person on the move, all excellent - even better if it is half price.

Chapter 4
KENYA for BUSINESS
SEA AND SAFARI

This was to be the first of our combined business and pleasure Travel, this trip was made before I had developed my two for one technique. It was booked through a high street travel agent but it was a standard end-of-season special offer. Not really special. It was for a one week holiday staying in the beautiful Indian Ocean Beach Club on the coast of Mombasa, Kenya and a second week was thrown in free of charge. The reason for the so-called offer was because it would be about the time for the start of the annual rains so naturally less people want to visit and bookings go down.

My intention was to have one weeks relaxation on the coast, swimming and sunning but at the same time I would purchase all the Kenyan newspapers and magazines that were available. These I would scan for likely or possible typewriter trading contacts. What I would be looking for mainly would be typewriter dealers plus schools, colleges and businesses. I also planned a trip to Mombasa town where I hoped to call on the typewriter dealer shops where I knew I would be made most welcome.

Kenya is in Eastern Africa. It borders Ethiopia in the north, Tanzania in the south, Somalia in the northeast, Uganda in the west, Sudan in the northwest and the Indian Ocean along it's southeast coast. So it is in the centre of much activity in this part of the world along with a fast growing population of 35 million, half of which are of school age.

Kenya in 2008 is a country with political troubles as is Zimbabwe and many other states throughout Africa. Tribal and political fighting flare up regularly as the Continent struggles to organise itself from its Colonial past to its new future.

In Africa tensions tend to arise quickly and subside slowly. Normally Kenya is a peaceful and beautiful country with pleasant people and sandy beaches, adding to that is the wonderful real life Wild Life. There are natural land areas throughout the country where animals live in a manner as nature designed them to live. These are lands free of mans intervention, apart from the camera-shooting tourists who go there to watch or study these wild animals that are set in a kind of time warp, each new day that these beasts of nature see is no different to the new day that was seen by their predecessors perhaps a million year ago.

One day this real natural world of nature could easily end as the quest for more and more land is sought by the ever

By day our lovely lodge, just yards from the sea, is considered the best lodge on the site.

27

growing and spreading band of humans.

The Masai Mara free game area is one of the world's finest and largest at over 600 square miles (1500 km²). It lies in the 3700 miles long (6000 km) Great Rift Valley running through Africa, this valley is thought to be the birth place of the first human beings Homo Erectus.

The journey from the airport to the Indian Ocean Beach Club was a real culture shock. This was our first trip to Africa. The heat and the humidity was just right, no problem there but the number of people seemed for a while to overtake our senses. We finally arrived at our Beach Club and was overwhelmed by its well designed and open spaced luxurious layout. It was all I was hoping for and more. I had studied in detail the holiday brochure pictures prior to booking the trip. The Beach Club consists of, I would guess, 100 or so individually spaced lodges and then the bars, restaurants and lounges. I remember thinking, at the time of booking, that I hoped I would get one of the lodges in the centre of the site. I felt that any lodge on the edge of the site could be a pretty easy target for break-in and theft. As it turned out we ended up with the best and potentially the worst lodge on the site. It was considered the best sited one because of its position right at the furthest point on the site and nearest the beach. That may sound lovely, cannot be better, that's on the good side. Unfortunately, on the bad side of things its position was like an outpost, not only on the site's boundary but also only a few yards from the beach. That sounds fine until you read the big signs which said KEEP OFF THE BEACH AT NIGHT - BEWARE OF THIEVES AND PIRATES. Now my way of reasoning is if I was a thief or pirate, an unprotected lodge about 20 yards from the beach edge would seem like easy pickings.

Sleep on the first night was a bit tricky to achieve with those thoughts in mind but there was something else adding to the drama. At night we draped our mosquito nets down and around the bed and as soon as the light went out he started up. We were aware we had an intruder in bed with us. No, it wasn't one of those thieves or pirates, it was worse than that. This was a multi-legged poisonous creature calling for its lost mate. Click, click, it went, a common calling cry, click, click, up went our nets on with the light, torches out but one hour later the unsuccessful hunt was abandoned. Let's leave it to fate we said so it was back into bed, lights out, nets down and click, click, he was at it again. I am not sure whether or not he found his mate or perhaps my hot feet rendered him unconscious whatever, sleep came upon us. The long travel and the fine wines did the trick. We woke up in the morning and seemed to be as before. No sign or sound was heard again from our visitor.

The next morning I was sitting outside our lodge taking in the early sun, when a young uniformed man approached me and introduced himself, with a "Good morning Sir, I am your nighttime guard and I am waiting for my daytime replacement, we meet on this corner to change shifts each day." We had a long chat and he explained that he was braver than the daytime guards. He seemed rather young and small to be able to ward off pirates but I was relieved to know there was at least an attempt to do so. After our long chat I offered him a packet of cigarettes as a thank you for his role in looking after us. "Thank you sir," he said and threw me a salute and off he went. The following morning whilst taking advantage of the morning sun, once again the guard, who we had nicknamed Shorty, turned up with his daytime replacement who he introduced to me. A cordial conversation took place for a while and when it was time for them to leave I presented both of them with a goodwill gift of a packet of cigarettes as a thank you. The second guard we nicknamed Lofty for obvious reasons. The next morning Shorty was not around but Lofty turned up with his "Good Morning Sir," and a salute. With him was guard No. 3. who we named Tough Guy, again, for obvious reasons. He introduced Tough Guy to me as the day guard who patrolled the other side of the site that terminated in my lodge corner. Apparently my corner position was the turning point of their patrolling. Again, I handed out the now customary daily packet of cigarettes. That evening as the guards changed their shift, (as I expected) I was introduced to another guard nicknamed No. 4 as he had no particular dimensions to refer to. I am now funding the smoking habit of four guards, two night and two daytime, all presenting themselves with the usual "Good Morning," or "Good Evening Sir," and that salute. That was fine by me but I was unsure my supply of cigarettes would last. I had purchased a number of cartons of duty-free cigarettes to use in this manner but I was now going through eighty a day. Still they were nice fellows so I was only too pleased to do this.

My thoughts on this changed slightly one day as I was leaving my lodge to walk the twenty yards or so to the beach. This was mid-morning and I said to Elizabeth: "I am off to take some photographs of the beach and the sea. Leaving the lodge and as I neared the beach, Tough Guy emerged from some thick bushes where he had been resting. "Good Morning Sir," and gave me the usual salute. As I walked on, he followed me and during our conversation, he began to discuss the equipment I had hanging around me. "That's a fine video camera you have Sir, is it worth much?". I went through some details of it as we walked on then: "That's is a nice camera Sir, is it worth much?" Again details were explained. A bit further on in our strolls: "Those binoculars look special. Are they worth much Sir?" Well by now I felt I was being valued. After all, without realizing it, I was carrying what would be a lot of wealth to a poorly paid African guard. Good binoculars, excellent camera, modern video camera, expensive watch, as we talked I had the uneasy feeling the temptation for the guards might be too much and maybe they were more of a threat than those pirates. Fortunately next morning we were to fly 300 miles up country.

Loading our Aircraft to take us to Masai Mara Country.

My intention when booking this Kenya trip back in the UK was that when in Kenya I would arrange locally, a flight up to the Masai Mara which is claimed to have some of the world's finest land areas free of mans hand and where nature and its wild animals act freely as they have done since the beginning of time. I arranged locally to take two seats in a small twin engined aircraft that came with a tired looking pilot who flew it with his knees whilst doing a crossword puzzle. A bit unnerving but we got there in one piece and all was well.

Our journey flew us over Mount Killimanjaro and on to our landing field in the Masai Mara plains. We were taken to our quarters which were to be in tents, now that may sound grim but these tents were superb, two beds, bathroom, wardrobes, all the features one would expect in a modern hotel room. Our tent was positioned 10 ft from the bank of the fast flowing Mara River which lay 20 ft below us in a gorge. A crocodile was lazily sunning itself on a lower ledge and in the water just below us was a gathering of 50 or so hippopotamis, a great spot to start our safari. Traditionally when on safari, one of the things to do is to log up the sighting of the "Big Five" mammals that means you become a spotter where you and your guide search them out and then you shoot them, not like the hunters of old who used guns, no we shoot them with our

The Big Five (Almost)

cameras.

The phrase "Big Five" was coined by big-game hunters and refers to five large mammals that were sought in Africa. The term is still used in most tourist and wildlife guides. The five consists of the lion, elephant, cape buffalo, leopard and the rhinoceros. The members of the Big Five were chosen for the difficulty in hunting them. They are among the most dangerous of the large mammals. The picture showing the five is running clockwise with the male lion with its heavy mane around its neck and shoulders, the elephant with its two tusks of ivory, the rhinoceros with its sought after horn, the Cape buffalo reported to be the most dangerous of the Big Five causing the most hunters' deaths and in the centre of the picture is a lazy leopard, a large carnivorous spotted feline.

Well, not quite, (all the photographs throughout the book are taken by myself) and my only leopard photo was taken in vegetation and is unclear, so I am afraid for the sake of the picture, I am cheating by using a cheetah instead which is a similar animal, a spotted feline but of smaller build than the leopard.

After settling in we meet our driver, Joseph and two other travellers who were to travel with us in an open top jeep type of vehicle. The safari camp was remote and therefore not restricted to road and routes. We were free to roam in our vehicle across open land through gullies, up hills everywhere, complete freedom to be able to seek out and study nature in its raw state and at its best, undisturbed by time.

I can remember on the first night sleeping in the tent was not easy. I woke Elizabeth suddenly by asking: "Did you sniff?" she replied "No". I said: "There must be a snake in here with us." So it was up with the nets and on with the lights. However, a subsequent search revealed nothing so it was back to sleep for a while. "Hello Sir," came a voice from nowhere. Again: "Hello Sir", I looked, blinked and stared, there was nothing to see but the black of the night. Suddenly I saw the source of "Hello Sir," it was just our African guide. "It is 5 o'clock sir," he said, "It is time for your early morning game drive," Pulling ourselves together we were soon dressed for the part and ready to go. We would take two game drives a day with Joseph, one early morning and the other mid afternoon in our quest to seek those living in this world of animals. The list of life is long, there are the elephants, giraffes, zebras, lions, cheetahs, leopards, buffalo, rhinos, ostriches, deer, wildebeast, hogs, hyenas to name a few. That is on the ground, then there is a mass of flying creatures in the air such as bats, eagles, songbirds, storks, vultures and other various birds of prey. These are the cleaners of the plains who aggressively eat

What do you do when dressed in lightweight clothing and sitting in our open top Jeep when suddenly this monster is heading your way.

33

up anything left to rot by the carnivores.

One day, during one of our jeep runs out in to the African plains, the sky began to darken and it was not long before a fearsome sight came over the horizon heading for us. A gigantic storm was coming our way and we were only dressed in summer gear in an open top jeep miles from home base. A good soaking we could survive, but lightning strikes and storm winds, that is not good, it looked like things are about to get a bit tough. The picture shows the green grass plains have turned black by loss of sunlight and seeing that, our fear factor started rising as we sat in the jeep not knowing which way to run. It became a decision we did not have to make, the winds decided for us as the vicious storm suddenly swerved away from us and our day was saved, as were we. Other days and other runs in our jeep showed us a continuous range of nature's magic with all the creatures of the land and the air, but there was also the life below the surface, the gigantic termite hills some 6ft high showing where these small creatures run there organised way of life.

Our few days living in the land of the wild animals was a time to remember and now was the time to fly back to our charming Indian Ocean Beach Club in Mombasa.

Arriving back at the Lodge, as I expected, we were met by our friendly guards, saluting and greeting our return.

The next day was a time to take our return flight home. We packed our bags and when the time came to leave, we opened the door to be met by, guess who? that's right, Shorty, Lofty, Tough Guy and No.4, our four guards who had come to wish us farewell. Well, of course, what they were really hoping for was a final tip and why not! I shook hands with them all and wished them all the best and gave them a handsome tip as a reward for their services.

Having survived the potential pillaging by pirates, the possibility of a rogue guard and not being eaten by lions, I felt we had accomplished a wonderful trip without too much drama. My thoughts however, were premature.

The flight back to London was fine. We arrived and landed late at night and whilst waiting for our luggage to come up the airport delivery system, I became aware of some laughter amongst other travellers who were also waiting for their luggage. An odd shoe suddenly came up the ramp followed by the odd sock. Other loose items then followed. We all laughed saying somebody is in trouble. It slowly dawned on me, I recognized these were my loose items. Suddenly my suitcase appeared which had been opened and robbed.

I had survived being turned into lunch by the lions, robbed by pirates and possibly guards, only to be plundered by some blighter at airport handling either in Mombasa or

London, I don't know which, but robbed I had been.

My losses were cameras and various other valuable bits and pieces. Although late at night, I made my losses clear to the Airport Police and then we had to deal with the drama of claiming from the insurance policies we took out for such situations. This was not as easy as one would expect. As with most insurance claims you are quickly made aware of the facts which usually amount to; "Sorry Sir you are not covered for that." My losses were in the order of £800, mostly video and camera items. I finally recovered these losses by having to claim a limited amount from the airline, a bit more from the travel insurance and some more from my general insurance cover.

On the business side of this visit. I gained a large quantity of information and understanding of Kenya, and I made contact with a number of managers that have now placed, over the last 15 years many orders for our reconditioned typewriters. In general these orders would be for 50 or 60 machines at a time, these we would send by air, direct to Nairobi Airport. They would usually be used to equip their typing classrooms in the various schools and colleges.

Chapter 5

ZIMBABWE

FOR BUSINESS AND PLEASURE

(Before The Troubles Began)

Our travel to Kenya had been a wonderful adventure and it also brought us into contact with a number of overseas business trading possibilities which is what I was hoping to achieve. Having had some success in this dual role of leisure and business, I decided to expand the idea to other countries. All I needed to do was to look for that special offer to the right place and we would give it a try.

Our next special offer was to Zimbabwe which is a country in the southern part of Africa between the Zambezi and Limpopo rivers. It borders South Africa in the south, Zambia in the north, Mozambique in the east and Botswana in the west. Our trip there was at a time before the country's economic collapse started and there was a lot on offer for the Tourists and the Business people. A situation that will hopefully return soon.

We flew out Club Class and stayed in what is claimed to be Africa's best hotel, the Mechels Hotel in Harrare the country's capital city. It was one of those special trips put together by a travel company to test the possibility of a new holiday for addition to their next year's brochure. They purchased all of the club class seats in the aircraft this, coupled with a good low price, ensured a quick sellout.

Zimbabwe was using the English keyboard so I knew exports were a good possibility. On arrival at the excellent Mechels Hotel, my first move, whilst Elizabeth was unpacking, was to reach for the Yellow Pages telephone directory and begin to note various typewriter dealers in the city. After some time I had produced a list of ten or so possible contacts. These I proceeded to telephone and discuss my range of machines that might suit their trading position. I had also taken out with me a number of sample packs showing the type of typewriters we could offer. I arranged appointments for these contacts to come and visit me in the hotel's business rooms where I was able to show and discuss our full range of machines. We meet with a number of worthwhile companies this way which over the course of time we have been fortunate to have received many orders to export machines to them.

One business idea I had was to prove unsuccessful. The idea was simple enough. I decided to look for a local Harrare company, one which I could team up with in the typewriter selling business. My plan was to hire a business premises where my potential colleague would be based.

The magnificent sight of nature at work. Water cascading 100's of feet
and forming a cloud of droplets that surround the area.

They could display a small stock of our machines but the main aim would be for him to make contact with schools and colleges and the like to obtain typewriter orders in quantity. Orders, thus obtained, we would despatch direct from our home-based workshop to the overseas customer. This sounds easy, however it was not to be. I was unable to make contact with the right company in the short time we were there.

On the pleasure side of the trip, it was very different to Kenya. For a start it is a land-locked country, so no sea or sand but plenty of adventures.

After all of my business contacts had been dealt with, we decided to relax and fly in a small aircraft a few hundred miles to see the great Victoria Falls, a waterfall between the borders of the two countries of Zambia and Zimbabwe.

The first European to see the falls was the explorer David Livingstone in November 1855. He gave them the English name of Victoria Falls in honour to his Queen Victoria, the African name is Mosi oa Tunya (the Smoke that Thunders). He wrote of the falls: It is hard to imagine the beauty of the scene. "It is a scene so lovely it must surely be gazed on by Angels in their flight". How right he was.

The falls have the honour to claim to have the largest sheet of falling water in the world where the whole Zambezi River, with a width of One mile (1.6km) and a height of 360ft (110 m) plummets in a single vertical drop into a deep chasm. The spray from the falls rises to a height over 1300ft (400 m) and is visible up to 30 miles (50 km) away. At night and with a full moon, a "Moonbow" can be seen in the spray as well as the daytime sun driven Rainbow.

For a few years now, due to political tensions on the Zimbabwean side, hotel occupancy is down to around 20% of what it was 10 years ago. This is due to mistaken political policies and tensions between supporters and opponents of President Robert Mugabe. Zimbabwe is in tatters; it is a country in economical ruin and despair. However one day the situation will change the country and its people will recover and when they do the falls will still be there in all its glory awaiting the return of the tourist. Meanwhile the Victoria Falls still remain one of Africa's major tourist attractions and is a UNESCO World Heritage Site, visited by more than 400,000 people a year, the majority from the Zambia side.

We flew back to our hotel in Harrare that evening after an exhilarating day of the sights and sounds of "the smoke that thunders."

The next afternoon was a lazy period spent just walking around town taking in the locals and the general scenes.

Whilst taking traditional afternoon tea in the hotel, we were approached by a pleasant man who introduced himself as one of the managers. During our chat his wife Winnie also arrived and joined us for tea. A pleasant hour was passed in this manner. We met the same man on a number of similar occasions during our stay. On the last day he approached me and asked if I would do him a favour. He asked me to purchase for him, when I was back in England, an anti wrinkle machine, which he wanted for his wife Winnie. Well, Winnie was getting on a bit and I reckoned it would have to be a pretty miraculous machine to tighten her tucks. I now realised that it was not a customer relations exercise that had been paying for our afternoon tea. However, it was not a difficult task to deal with and so I agreed. I just hope Winnie gained from it!

During our short stay in Zimbabwe, we managed to achieve and make contact with a number of worthwhile future trading businesses. We also managed a good variety of entertaining days such as, mentioned previously, flying up to see the great Victoria Falls. We also managed a day's Safari and other adventures such as canoeing up a crocodile infested tributary of the Zambezi river which sounds simple but when three people are put together in a canoe with no idea of what to do, life can get difficult. A young lady named Victoria was at the head of the canoe, Elizabeth midsection and I on the tiller. We all paddled off trying to keep up with the other five canoes. This was not to be, we ended up going in all directions but the right one. Eventually we got our act together with Victoria bellowing instructions on how to proceed. Elizabeth remained silent obviously fearing she would end up as lunch for some nearby crocodile but with my developing skills as the tiller man, we eventually overtook some of the other canoes and reached our destination. It was with great relief that we managed to engage land and place our feet on solid soil. We had paddled a long way, it seemed like miles, for a BBQ but this one had a difference to it. It was 30ft up in a big sprawling tree. We climbed the ladder and took our places at the table and chairs which were set out in the branches to cater for twenty or so people. The menu was a delight to read with a range of the unusual delicacies such as warthog sausages and buffalo burgers. We ate with a mixture of relief and hunger while the Zambezi crocodiles, I am glad to say, went hungry.

It was on our return from one of these day trips that our coach driver made an arranged stop at a stonemasons yard. The yard was full of African stone carvings, hundreds of them, all shapes and sizes and various art styles traditional African right through to the Modern art styles. As our coach group of some fifty people were walking around the yard making the odd choices to buy this or that, I suddenly spotted her. What a beauty she is, I immediately thought. No, no not the receptionist, no this was Esmerelda an amazing carving almost full size of a young woman. She was covered in dust and looking neglected but to me this was real art and I new how much skill was needed to produce such a three dimensional beautiful object. I knew I would buy this overlooked beauty but no price was to be seen so I trekked off to the office and asked the price £180 was the reply. Right, time to collect the carving we have come to know as Esmerelda and take her to the office to haggle over the final price. When I returned to where she had been resting for goodness knows how long, I was shocked to see another couple had fallen for her. They were almost at the point of agreeing to buy her. I realised I had to act quickly, I needed to create a diversion. Standing near this couple, I called out to some friends nearby; "Have you seen those great multi-colour carvings over there on the far side?" Fearing they had missed something special, my competitors moved off to see what was to be had. That was it, Esmerelda was now secured by me, and quickly taken to the pay office where I finally purchased her for £120. Even after a number of years with us, I still study this carving almost daily for its expert work and fine detail and I seem to sense a knowing smile.

ESMERELDA

Found in the dust of a stonemason's yard.

Beautifully carved by MURAMBIKA OF Kenya.

Chapter 6

BARBADOS for BUSINESS and BEACHES

Barbados is only a small Coral Island but a good special flight offer was there to be had, so as they use the English qwerty keyboard we decided to take it and do another business and leisure trip.

This was another of those experimental one-off trips arranged by the travel company. It was for one week in a top Barbadian hotel and travelling the long flight in club class, yet the price asked was less than many European trips.

Barbados is situated east of the Caribbean Sea, an island in the Western Atlantic Ocean. The island is well developed, and there are internationally known hotels offering first class accommodation. The Southern and Western coasts of Barbados are popular, with the calm warm light blue Caribbean sea and fine white sandy beaches. Along the island's east coast the Atlantic Ocean side, are strong tumbling waves which are used with much joy by the surfers.

Shopping districts are popular with duty-free shopping.

There is an active night life in many tourist areas. Other attractions include wildlife reserves, scuba diving, golf to play, caves to explore, exotic drinks and food to savour and plenty of rum and emeralds to shop for.

The climate is tropical, with a rainy season from June to October and the wind blowing off the Atlantic Ocean serve to keep temperatures mild, so quite a nice place to go to.

Barbados history is that British sailors landed on the Island in 1625 and found it uninhabited, as a result British farmers were recruited and they began to arrive in 1628 bringing with them workers sent by King James II, these were Irish, Scots and English, they were white slave workers. Often referred to as Indentured Servants, but they were taken there against their will as a punishment. Black slave workers followed. The population grew from a large number of Celtic people in the seventeenth century into an overwhelming number of African people by the nineteenth century. The population is now over 300,000.

Here are a few interesting local customs:

*Barbados has one of the highest standards of living and literary rates in the world despite its small size.

*It is an offence for anyone, even a child to wear camouflage clothing.

*The drinking age in Barbados is 18, but ages of between 10 to 17 can join in if with a parent.

BEAUTY AND THE BARBADOS BEACHES
The Caribbean is famed for its beaches and sun with shops
full of rum and emeralds.

*The British system of Longitude was discovered by charting the distance between Portsmouth, England and Bridgetown, Barbados, using the sun in relation to both locations.

Armed with an understanding of the Island and the offer of a good value flight and hotel package, we decided to take to the sky, however things are not always as planned.

It's a long flight to Barbados and this would normally be too long for my restless legs, so when this flight offer using club class seat spacing came up I decided this would suit me and we would give it a try.

At the airport, as we booked in, that common cry came up: "sorry Sir," and went on to explain," your aircraft has been grounded for technical reasons. However, the company has arranged for a replacement aircraft but unfortunately it has no club class seating "sorry Sir".

I thought 10 or 11 hours in those cramped-up seats, I am not looking forward to that, however came the soft voice, we are providing all the club class passengers with two seats each instead, I hope that is alright sir? I replied it's not what I was expecting but it's better than walking, so book us in.

Our week in Barbados soon passed, on arrival home I reflected on the journey. It had been mainly a week of leisure with the fine beaches and sun, and the odd tourist trip to the rum plantations, along with hunting in the shops for a special buy. Elizabeth managed to purchased a large emerald ring and I a large supply of rum.

On the business side I made contact with several companies and typewriter dealers which have proved very worthwhile. It was a long journey but it was a pleasant one week special offer.

I was finding our foreign travel exciting and rewarding having completed several trips.

These were at a time when Concorde was flying, and I like most other people had a great longing to fly super-sonic in it. As we know anyone could, all you had to do was pay the price of the ticket, however it was to expensive for most peoples pocket, including mine.

I became aware that several tour companies' would often Charter Concorde from BA and arrange a special flight along with a weeks holiday to an exotic place. I also found that to fill empty seats late booking could sometimes get a high discount up to 50%, which meant that two people went for the price of one. Now that seemed to me to be a good idea and one I should know more about and take up.

The next six Tales of Travel are Concorde journeys taken this way. The first, full of excitement and awe, is off to the ice laden Arctic and Greenland.

SOMEWHERE OVER GREENLAND

Viewed through the window of Concord flying on the edge of space. Height 60,000ft speed 1400mph. First there is Concord's wing then the snow capped mountains of Greenland, the white glow of the Ice Cap under the various coloured layers of our Planet's Atmosphere, Stratosphere, Ionosphere and the deep Black of Space.

44

Chapter 7

CONCORDE TO GREENLAND

Exports to Greenland! "You must be joking," said one of the mechanics, "there is hardly anyone living there." My reply was: "I have exported typing machines to the Falklands and there are a lot less people there." The reason for this discussion about Greenland was brought about by my noticing that one of the travel companies I use had a Concorde trip coming up soon, and it only flies to Greenland once a year. Elizabeth had seen this trip advertised in the travel company's brochure and remarked that it seemed a nice place to go to. My thoughts to start with were the opposite - cold, ice, snow - that seemed pretty grim to me. My view changed suddenly when at very short notice I managed to book another special bargain a (two for one deal).

The Concorde to Greenland trip resulted in us having a quick dash to the nearest hikers/bikers shop where we purchased a range of keep warm gear which included our mountain boots and thermal underwear. We were now ready to go, which was to be only three days later.

This journey was like no other, to be able to travel to the Arctic was exciting but to be taken there in Concorde, at twice the speed of sound as well, was like a dream, and this was to a world of ice and snow where, for many, their means of travel is by Dog power.

The Island of Greenland borders the Atlantic Ocean on its south coast, the Greenland Sea on its east coast, Baffin Bay on its west coast, and the Arctic Ocean on its north coast. It is the World's largest island, most of it ice covered .

The Greenland ice cap covers 680,000 square miles (1,750,000 square kilometres), over 80 per cent of its land mass. The weight of the ice cap, it is said, is so massive it has depressed the centre of this, the world's largest island to form a huge basin more than 1000 ft (300 m) deep below sea level. It has also been said that if this ice cap melts away with global warming, the world's sea level will rise 23ft (7 m).

The Supersonic Concorde flight (now grounded) was, out of this world, so high, so fast, so smooth, this is because it flew above our weather atmosphere and was free of turbulence. It was the perfect flying machine in every aspect. The view out of the window could be magic always changing depending on what part of the world we were flying over and what time of day or night it was.

Inside we would gaze in awe at the large Altitude and Speed display panels high on the front wall of each cabin. The excitement could be felt and the sound of cheers was heard as we went through the Sound Barrier at (Mach 1) and again - only on this passenger aircraft did it happen - more cheers when the display reaches (Mach 2) which is 1350 mph when flying at 60,000 ft.

At the speed of sound an invisible barrier is formed by the compressibility of air, a force many experts believed could not be flown through, and there were to be many brave test pilots who died trying. It was considered man's final frontier in aviation until the first aviator broke through it and lived to tell the tale.

As the aircraft breaks through this barrier a sonic boom is created sending a shock wave a loud thunder type of noise in strength, down unto the earth. It is for this reason Supersonic flight is only undertaken over sea or approved land areas.

The speed sound travels at sea level is 762 mph (1225 kph) and it is affected by altitude and temperature. Concorde was designed to fly at 60,000 ft where the outside air temperature is minus 50° C. Here it exceeds the speed of 1350 mph (2170 kph) which is twice the speed of sound, ie MACH 2 .

I remember as a young man each year we would cycle a 100 miles to spend the day at the Farnborough Flying Airshow. In those days in order to entertain us and for the jet fighter aircraft to become supersonic the pilot would dive his aircraft from a high altitude aiming directly at the airfield. We would all hear and feel the sonic boom produced as the Jet broke though the sound barrier.

One year, a "de-Haviland 110" aircraft broke up in its dive and began to disintegrate, killing the two man crew. The pilot John Derry, who was the first British pilot to break the sound barrier, and navigator Tony Richards.

The two large Rolls Royce engines tore free, one, screaming over the heads of the packed crowds, fell safely, the other headed straight towards us as it bore down onto the main viewing hill that was packed solid with spectators who had nowhere to run to. It ploughed its way through leaving in its wake 30 killed and nearly 100 injured, plus 120,000 others around the airfield in a state of stunned shock, for they knew, each one of them, that it could have been them laying there.

One hour later, despite the terrible carnage still on the ground, flying resumed with test pilot Nevill Duke in a Hawker Hunter jet fighter performing another supersonic dive and a corkscrew roll just clear of the runway, as a mark of respect to the fallen, and an act of defiance to the infamous barrier.

These tough test pilots showed the world that mankind was strong enough to go through the sound barrier, even if the aircraft of the day were not.

I expect most of the people that flew in Concorde were more concerned with their Lobsters and Champagne than knowing about the flight history and the amazing technology that made the construction and flying of this aircraft possible. But by not knowing the facts, they could not experience the real deep thrill of supersonic flying that lay with the knowing.

After landing at Kangerlussuaq, a major airport on the west coast, we all quickly transferred to two small, piston engine aircraft to fly us several hundred miles further north, deeper into the Arctic, where we landed at an airfield close to our hotel, it was based in a small town of 4,000 people and 6,000 dogs.

PHOTO---During the winter days dog sleighs are for many people the only means of travel.
The bitch and her cute pup are enjoying their summer break and the sun as they look down onto the harbour.

Within an hour of booking into our rooms, we had changed into our keep warm gear and were whisked off to a nearby helliport. There we boarded one of the Greenlandair helicopters for our flight up to the ice cap and one of the larger ice fjords.

After landing on a high stoney edge we all walked around gazing in awe at the sight of this massive ice fjord, some 25 miles long and 5 miles wide.

I could not help thinking only a few hours ago we were in London and now having flown on the edge of space, faster than a rifle bullet and whilst up there we were sipping champagne and eating the finest foods in absolute comfort. Nobody else travelled as high and fast apart from a few fighter pilots and astronauts and there is no champagne for them!

We are now in the Arctic and gazing in wonder at this spectacle of nature's might. However, it was not long before we had the call to return to our helicopter.

As we lifted off to take us back to our base, we flew across the glassier's shear iceface (see photo). This face is where icebergs are created as they break away from the main ice sheet, it is called calving and the sea area, where they first gather ready for their new life as they push out to sea, is known as a nursery. This massive moving iceface stands 300ft (100m) above sea level with a further 2,700 ft(900m)

A 300ft (100m) wall of ice above and around 3000ft (1000m) below Sea Level.

ILULISSAT / JAKOBSHAVN
GREENLAND

ICECAP

Certificate

This is to certify that

Mrs. E. Everest
NAME

flew up

ILULISSAT *ice fiord*
on a Greenlandair
helicopter

PILOT IN COMMAND

GL 6718
FLIGHT NO.

04. June 1997
DATE

Ilulissat
Tourist=
Service

INFORMATION ABOUT THE FLIGHT

The Jakobshavn ice fiord is 40 kilometers long by 7 kilometers wide. It is believed to be fed by the most productive glacier in the world, producing around 20 million tons of ice every day.

The ice begins moving 600 kilometers inland, up at 3000 meters. It is then squeezed out down the coastal ice fiords. Jakobshavn ice fiord is the fastest of these, moving at almost one meter each hour. Here at Jakobshavn two ice streams come together. The northern flow is moving at eight meters a day, whilst the southern flow moves at twenty two meters each day. They become fused together and at the calving front the movement is at twenty two meters a day.

The front calves once every two to four weeks. At this time the frontal face moves back between three and five kilometers.

As a general rule the ice coming from the northern side of the front breaks into smaller pieces, while the large ice bergs come from the southern side.

The fiord depth at the calving front is about 1500 meters with an ice depth of around 1000 meters. 70-100 meters of this is above the water with the remainder below sea level. The last 12 kilometers of this is floating, with a rise and fall almost 3 meters with the tide.

The ice temperature is at a constant minus 10° C, except at the base. There it is heated by friction with the rock to around zero, so the flow of the ice is lubricated by water.

There is a ridge at the mouth of the ice fiord, where the depth decreases to about 200 meters. The smaller bergs float very rapidly out in to the Disco Bay, but the large bergs can take up to two years to break up small enough to float over the ridge and away south into the Atlantic. All the large bergs that you see in the mouth of the fiord are resting on the bottom. Ice floats about 9/10 under water.

We will be landing up at the ice front and stopping the helikopter for about 30 minutes. If you have any questions please do not hesitate to ask the crew at the time.

Please relax and enjoy your trip with us, we hope it will be an experience to remember.

below sea level, this mass of ice constantly heads down into the sea travelling at 22m (70 ft) a day. However global warming is causing the ice to slip faster each year. It has been reported that it has now reached over 100 ft a day.

After arriving back at our hotel it was time for me to do some work, so I immediately made business calls to a number of contacts and officials to discuss the possible sales of our range of writing machines to them.

Greenland has it own language but many speak Danish as it is a Danish colony. However, as all around the world much business is done in the English language so the potential of a sales market, although limited, still exists, also English is widely used as a second language. After consulting and considering all the facts and figures and realising the population is mainly in small locations all around the island's vast coastline and therefore very widespread, the setting up of a sales market would prove too difficult to be practical.

So it was time for a bit more leisure. This tour operator had a continuous range of events to keep us all happy, one of these was the 24 hour midnight sun cruise among the array of newly formed icebergs. So back at the hotel, on went the thermal's although it was a nice warm day, no night, only minus 5°c but temperatures can drop suddenly aided by the wind chill factor to minus 35°c. On with all the other keep warm gear and it was off to the docks where a flotilla of small boats were warming up their engines ready to take all 100 of us out to sea. I had been fearing this part of our trip as I am a bad sailor, the slightest rolling motion and I begin to get poorly. I feared the worst but it was not to be. The new freshwater icebergs created on their merging with the salty sea water, a kind of tranquil smoothie. The mixed sea water was, as they say, as smooth as a mill pond. To be able to travel in this way to see this world of ice, a world that by its existence controls all our destiny, is incredible.

During our cruise all five of our small boats came together at the side of one of these icebergs for a midnight in the sun celebration champagne drink with pieces of cooling ice snapped off the nearby freshwater iceberg - not all that fresh probably 10,000 years old, but we all survived to tell the tale. Whilst sipping our iced champagne, seemingly out of nowhere, came another small boat similar to ours. This boat was carrying a surprise mid-sea entertainment group. The local Inuit village singing group were on board and in the middle of this midnight sun, iceberg laden sea, they proceeded to give us an hour of very pleasant music and singing, sometimes interrupted by the cracking noise of bergs as they calved or split. After the champagne and canapes, and the singers were off to their beds, it was time

CRUISE IN THE MIDNIGHT SUN

One of our boats racing back to port and passing the craggy berg on the left and on the right a huge grounded berg rounded by the sun.

for our return to the harbour and our hotel. As we raced back at full speed, each boat trying to be the first, we were glad of our trip to the hikers/bikers shop. This was where our keep warm gear was most needed, the fast motion of our boats brought the wind chill temperature down to -35°c. My camera as usual, had been busy. On our return home I studied the prints and decided to offer the travel company the use of some of them. Whilst I keep the copywrite, they were offered these to use free of charge. I am pleased to say they took up my offer, one of which, showing the boat and the bergs, was used in their national press adverts and also in their glossy brochure. This picture of a boat and two bergs shows the boat between one berg craggy and new and another older berg that had grounded and was being rounded by the sun, this ice berg will remain stuck until the sun has reduced its size and mass such that it can float free and move on to its destiny.

After many other exciting events, it was time to head for home so it was back to the airport for all 100 of us to take our seats in the Queen of the Sky with the usual excitement and anticipation. As we all settled down there was a sudden announcement. A refined voice introduced himself with the normal courtesies but then added that there was a mountain ahead of the runway and he was going to make sure we got over it. These words of reassurance were coming from our pilot, they were words that would numb the senses of many travellers anywhere, but things here were different.

We were in the ice laden Arctic at Kangerlussuaq, an ex-World War 2 American airfield and our pilot was in charge of one of the most powerful flying machines ever made. He continued to explain how he was going to get us over this mountain. He said: "I am going to do something I could not do anywhere else in the world, I am taking off on full engine power and also full afterburner power. This procedure is banned around the world due to the restrictions on noise control levels, but as there are more people on this aircraft than on the ground in and around this airfield, that is what I intend to do." I think to most people that statement must have had an element of excitement about it. In my case, whilst on the one hand I was thrilled to be party to such a rare high powered event, after all, almost everyone loves the feel of rapid acceleration, the faster it is the greater the thrill felt, on the other hand I was also numbed by what the pilot was planning to do. He was without realising, putting the aircraft under an incredible amount of stress and strain. Using all this awesome intense power to accelerate Concorde to its takeoff speed of 250 mph as quickly as possible from a standing start which meant to move the

PREPARING FOR DEPARTURE FLIGHT

Ground Crew are preparing Concorde for our return flight from from Greenland at a mile every 2½ seconds. This is a rare picture of Concorde in service without its usual painted coloured tail fin and side stripes.

combined weight of 100 people and with the aircraft's hold full of luggage, the fuel tanks filled to the brim, plus the weight of the aircraft. To get to move all this weight so fast on full engine power plus the full thrust of the afterburners could possibly shred the tyres or even result in an engine tearing loose and maybe away from the wing. It is a rare thing to occur but occur it does.

After my 6 year apprenticeship in the aircraft industry as a young man I then served two years in the Royal Air Force Transport Command, working on a wide variety of large aircraft. During this two year span we had four aircraft land with engines that had partially torn away from their wing fixing bolts and these engines although powerful were nothing like the power of Concorde engines. However, despite my excitement and knee-knocking thoughts, the design of Concorde's engine mounting bolts held good as they should and proved capable of being able to take our full load at this very high powered, extremely fast and heavily loaded takeoff and, as a result, the mountain was cleared and a fantastic supersonic flight back to London was had by all on board.

However! I sometimes wonder, was there really a dangerous mountain there to get over, or was this, for the air crew, in this cold, frozen, isolated place, one of those moments in time when one senses and seizes an opportunity?

After all, it must have been every Concorde pilot's dream that when in the control seat of this, the world's fastest airliner ever built, he would (one day) have the possibility to be able to accelerate the aircraft and all 100 of us on board into the sky, using the full force and power of the four magnificent Rolls Royce engines that were at his finger tips.

As this is probably the only place in the world where they could do it without a massive public protest, I think the opportunity would have been seized.

The maximum power of the four is awesome, and in this most rare and isolated place the temptation to use them would be enormous, and almost impossible to resist.

Our membership cards to a Rare Club! We are supersonic Mach 2 members, No 2119 & 2120.

Chapter 8

CONCORDE AND CAIRO

Business for us in North Africa seemed very unlikely but we were now working with and supplying a large number of business contacts we had made in Southern Africa and West Africa. Therefore, when a nice sounding trip to North Africa presented itself, I decided to check it out and do another leisure come business-seeking trip, this time it would be to Egypt and Nubia.

This trip was a special, put together by one of my chosen travel companies and they offered club class on Egypt Air to Cairo and British Airways Concorde return to London. It was one of those travel trips to test the appetite of the public. It was a good offer and sold out quickly.

After taking off from Heathrow Airport, London, we headed for Cairo, the capital of Egypt, where for a few days we soaked up the atmosphere of tombs and temples galore, all beautiful and breathtaking with its thousands of year's of history. One of our Cairo tourist stops was to be at one of the Seven Wonders of the World, the Giza Pyramids where we stand in awe at such a work of man. The picture shows the Great Pyramid of Cheops which is among the world's largest man-made structures .

The Cheops Pyramid was built between 2589-2566 BC. It took over 2,300,000 giant stone blocks with an average weight of 2.5 tons each to make this massive monument. The total weight is around 6,000,000 tons and it stands 482 feet (140m) in height. It is thought it took 100,000 slaves and peasant workers over 30 years to build, this, the King's Pyramid, the largest of three standing on the site.

The (insert) in the picture shows Cheops has a descending passage which leads to an underground chamber. This long tunnel slopes down at a steep angle that descends deeply into the ground beneath the massive Pyramid. The passageway is low and narrow. It can be quite a difficult and claustrophobic task for some people but a task well worth taking if you can.

In my case, I reached the bottom and the chamber where I become a part of a small crowd. Looking back up the long small narrow tunnel I could see daylight and it was not long before I decided, that is where I should be. The thought of a possible coach-load of tomb loving Tibetian tourists heading down the tunnel to jam us in was beginning to adjust my stress levels. As I made it out I felt relived and good, extremely good, that I had travelled the tunnel into Cheops Tomb, a tunnel dug so deep under one of the world's most massive monuments built so long ago, over 45 centuries back in time.

THE GREAT PYRAMID AT GIZA

This man made miracle over 3500 years old, can overwhelm the senses but even more so when descending the steep low passage into the inner depths of this wonder (insert).

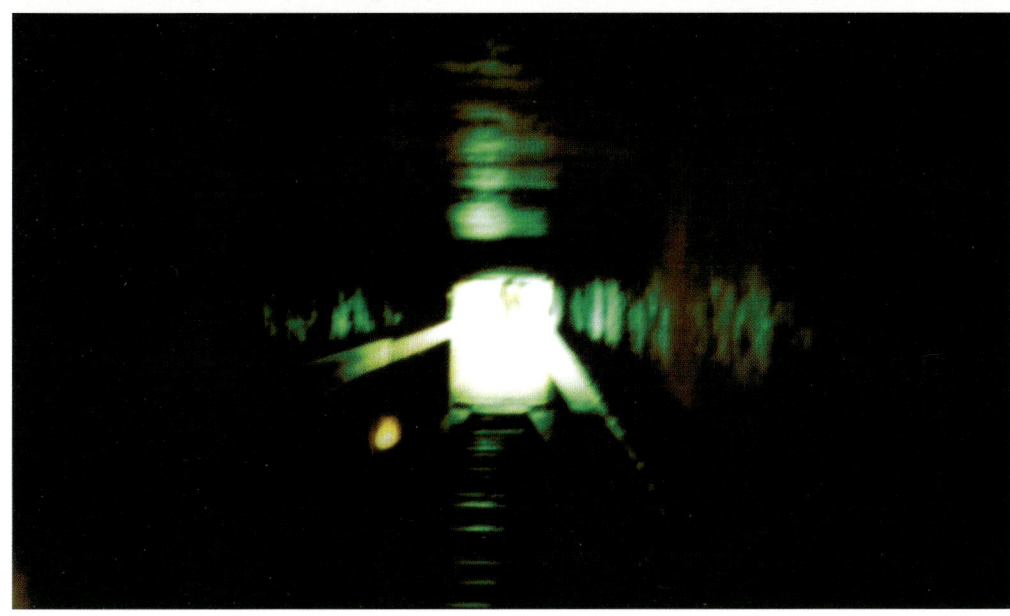

Light at the end of the Tunnel
almost half-way out.

After a few days in this marvellous city of Cairo we flew south down to the town of Aswan and were then taken by coaches to board our boat, the Eugenie, which was moored on the southern side of the great Aswan Dam. This was the part of the Nile which had flooded and formed Lake Nasser after the dam was built. On board ship everything was charming and elegant and for three days we cruised 280K down to our target destination which were the two temples of the Pharaoh Rameses II and his favourite wife, Nefertari, constructed at Abu Simbel in Nubia.

During the cruise we would stop at other various ancient sites which had survived the flooding. As the water level rose almost all life was wiped out, this was caused by the fact that these are very hot desert lands where life mainly exists along the side of the Nile and only reaches a small way inland, so as the water rose the banks became submerged and consigned to the new deep waters leaving, in most places, fresh banks consisting of nothing but a barren moon-like landscape.

The scene in the photo which was taken from our boat Eugenie as it approached Abu Simbel in the distance, might not look very impressive, it is only when you are close up or inside that the marvel becomes overwhelming.

The recent history of the Temples is that it was considered such an important part of our world history it had to be saved. So in order to save it from these rising waters that would overwhelm it, the whole temple was cut into 807 blocks with an average weight of 20 tons each, and with great difficulty taken up 190 ft (60m) to higher ground where it was reassembled. That was a modern marvel in itself and considered to be one of the greatest feats of archaeological engineering ever. It was a four year UNESCO project completed in 1968 and costing 80 million dollars. That action saved this site for all of us now, and our future generations to see and wonder at.

The Pharaoh Rameses II was a prolific builder of temples and monuments. This one is built on the edge of his empire and presents a frontage 125ft wide and 100ft tall

M S EUGENIE

The ship Eugenie became our floating hotel for a week as it took us in great comfort the 280K through hot desert lands to the Nubian Temple at Abu Simbel. The insert on the right are the elegantly designed interdeck stair well and on the left one of the charming lounge bars.

ABU SIMBEL

Approaching the temple from the lake and the insert on the left is the wall plaque commemorating the saving of Abu Simbel and on the right a dawn sunrise glow on the face of Ramses II.

with four 67ft high images of himself. It is thought it was built as a deterrent to ward off other lesser skilled warring nations who might think about sailing North up the Nile to plunder Egypt. It was built around 1284 BC and with the passing of time, the temples were almost lost from sight by being covered with the wind-blown moving desert sands. These abandoned temples were forgotten by the world for over 3,000 years until a local boy named Abu Simbel led the Swiss explorer and orientalist, J. L. Burckhardt, to the site in 1813. He in turn told the Italian explorer, Giovanni Belzoni, who in 1817 finally succeeded in digging a way into the main temple. In order to aid his exploration Burckhardt took the name Sheikh Abdallah and then spent two years in the Levent learning to become a master of Arabic. He proceeded on a series of exploration trips in the region, one of these led to the discovery of the Rose Red City of Petra in Jordan, which had lay hidden for a 1000 years. Further searching journeys took him into Nubia where he travelled disguised as a poor Syrian merchant, here he revealed to the world this lost for 3000 years Temples of Rameses II.

His major quest in Africa had been to try and find the source of the River Niger this eventually took him back to Cairo to join a huge caravan of people and animals preparing to depart and take the route South. Before he had the chance to accompany this caravan pulsing with life and excitement, fate and the grim reaper stood in his path, so it was not to be. Johann Ludwig Burckhardt died of dysentery in 1817 at the sad young age of 33 years. Such a brave body of a man along with a marvellous mind cut down so soon, but his amazing discoveries are now exposed for us all to wonder at, and thrill over with admiration, forever, or until time takes its toll.

Today thousands of tourists visit these temples daily. Armed guarded convoys of buses and cars depart twice daily from the town of Aswan 280K away. Others arrive by plane at a specially constructed local airfield and some, like us, by boat.

The complex consists of two Temples. The larger one is dedicated to Ra Harakhty, Ptah, Amun and Rameses. The smaller temple is dedicated to the Goddess Hather and Nefertari, Rameses main beloved wife. She was 13 years old and Rameses 15 when they married. Nefertari means beautiful companion, the name he gave his young wife.

She is one of the best known Egyptian Queens next to Cleopatra. After her death poetry written by Rameses about his special wife adorns the wall of her burial chamber: "My love is unique, no one can rival her for she was the most beautiful woman just by passing, she has taken away my heart."

Rameses gave his lost and so beloved soul mate, his special woman a last gift, all he had left to give her, which was to be that of the grandest of tombs.

This he had built for her in a style befitting his special Queen the finest and most beautiful resting place, still to be seen lying with 80 other tombs in the Valley of the Queens. This Valley is located on the West Bank of the River Nile across from the ancient Temple of Luxor.

The great Abu Simbel Temple took 20 years to build and is generally considered the grandest and most beautiful in Egypt. The precise positioning of the temple by the Egyptian architects is, in such a way, that twice a year at the Solstice, rays of sunlight penetrate through the large open front doors at 5.58 am on October 21st and again on February 21st. The rays of the sun stream in to illuminate the Sacrarium, 215ft deep inside the temple reaching the back wall where there are four seated sculptures of Ra Harakhti, Rameses, Amum Ra and Ptah. The sun's rays would glow only on three of the four as one, Ptah the God connected with the underworld, the Lord of the Darkness, must always remain in the dark.

The Temples' entombment by the shifting sands meant much of the interior is well preserved, the sculptured Gods, the wall-carved scenes of battles, even coloured paintworks of Egyptology on the walls. Whilst outside every morning at sunrise, as the sun breaks the Eastern horizon, the front face of the temple and the four huge statues of Rameses change colour and take on a golden glow, announcing to the world that the Gods have allowed another new day to start.

Most of the travellers coming to see this site plan to arrive early to mid-morning as the afternoon temperatures can be excessive and dangerously hot. It can mean that at peak times, it can be crowded, but for us boat people, we were in a favourable position. We kicked off early just before dawn to see the sunrise and to beat the crowds.

After several hours in the hot sun we returned to our cabin for refreshments. It was then that I decided, heat or not, when the crowds had reduced in the afternoon, that I must go back as I had forgotten to take my camera with me during our early morning trip and there were scenes and sights waiting to be captured. As it turned out, it was to be quite an amazing time for the two of us. Mid-afternoon, Elizabeth and I decided to do a quick visit from our moored boat. We headed for the Temple with camera tightly in hand, It was only then that we were to realise that the whole site was clear of people. Whilst we had expected it to be quiet, with the thousands dropping to perhaps hundreds this was a shock, not a soul in sight anywhere. Perhaps we should have seen this as a warning. However,

ON TOP OF THE TEMPLE
AT ABU SIMBEL

Looking down from the top we see our lake cruiser and the enchanting blue of the Nile and the distant hills of Nubia.

we pressed on and managed to keep out of the direct heat from the sun's rays by quickly moving from one shadow to another whenever it was possible and the reward to us was that we had this ancient site to ourselves, a marvellous feeling.

After a while, although we would now be exposed to the full sun, we decided to risk it and take the long steep climb up a rocky path on to the top of the temple. This enabled us to see and absorb the beauty of the scene and I was able to take the picture (a bit hazy due to the heat) showing our boat moored at the foot of the site, the blue waters of the Nile and the almost lifeless distant grey hilltops of Nubia. Below us was the temple's frontage, this, the people gathering area is empty whereas a few hours previously it was teeming with tourists. Even on our boat the top deck is clear the sundeck and the swimming pool are empty, not a sign of life anywhere.

This World heritage, UNESCO rescued site of Rameses II, considered to be one of the most magnificent ancient monuments visited daily by thousands, was ours and ours alone for a brief moment in time.

There are not many people in the world who could lay claim to such a sensuous moment. Even Rameses himself could not have experienced the silence, solitude and sights from this high spot. He would have been surrounded by an assembly of servants and followers, so for us two to be in this rare position, despite the scorching sun and the high temperatures of around 130°f and the steep climb to the top of the temple, to be able to capture this picture of isolation with not a single other soul in sight, was well worth the effort.

From all our world travels, that afternoon of having Rameses Temple to ourselves, for that brief moment in time, is probably our "finest moment in time anywhere."

On our return down to the front viewing area, I took the picture showing Elizabeth standing between Rameses 3 and Rameses 4. This is the same spot where the film star Mia Farrow stood in the film of Agatha Christie's book "Death on the Nile."

The second Rameses was damaged by earth tremors with the upper part falling during the 34th year of Rameses 67 year reign and has lain on the ground ever since. It must have been a sad blow to Rameses and all his team of builders to see their marvellous skilled work damaged so soon after taking 20 years to complete it. They probably looked upon it as a warning from one of their Gods.

The next day after another viewing of the dawn sunrise and the golden glow onto the temples, the Eugenie with us on board set sail back to Aswan. From there we would fly back to Cairo, a further 530 miles away.

The four great statues of Ramses II showing how big they are in comparison to Elizabeth standing in between No.3 and 4.

CONCORDE IN CAIRO

The finest Air Ship of the Sky and insert, the finest Ship of the Desert, both means of transport, both supreme in each one's world. One has come briefly and has now gone, the other will be here for ever.

On arrival in Cairo we had plenty of time before our London return home flight, to have one last desert lunch together. We were first of all booked into the Mena House Hotel for a freshen-up. A couple of hours later, we were taken back to the Pyramids and out into the desert for a late lunch in a Bedouin style tent with fine food and traditional entertainment.

Finally, after all the excitement, it was time to think of flying home but this was to be exciting as well, as our return to London was on Concorde. It was often quoted that one of the most desired things to do when people were asked was to fly supersonic in Concorde.

Our return take-off time was early evening and this was a Sunday. Now Sunday evenings to me are a bit special, about 9.30p.m. I join half a dozen men friends in our local pub for a pint and a good chat about this and that. I had calculated that without hold-ups and if the pilot puts his foot down, I might just make it back home in time for my Sunday night pint at the pub. It only takes just over three hours for Concorde to get us to London from Egypt. Then a fast taxi ride home from the airport followed by a quick case of unloading the luggage and paying the driver, then I am off, making a dash for the pub.

After such an intense day of travelling I arrived at 9.32 pm, just 2 minutes late. As I stood at the bar chatting about this and that, I glanced down and spotted the state of my shoes, they were still thickly covered with the dust and sand from the Egyptian desert thousands of miles away. I suddenly realised what a day this had been!

We had started it, with an excellent breakfast in Nubia whilst we were floating down Lake Nasser as we headed for Aswan. Then a few hours later, after flying from Aswan airport to Cairo in Egypt, an exotic lunch was taken in a Bedouin tent near the ancient pyramids.

And later that day, we were off to Cairo airport as it was now time to head for London. During the flight a superb (fine dining) champagne dinner was served, whilst we were flying supersonic in the incredible Concorde 10 miles high in the sky, and so fast, (a mile nearer home every two and a half seconds.)

And now I was back on the ground in the evening and I am in England having a perfect pint in my local pub with good friends.

What a day! Breakfast in Nubia, lunch in Egypt, dinner Supersonic high in the sky, and now an English pint in the evening

That I reckon, to anyone's measure must count as a "pretty good day!"

Chapter 9
CONCORDE TO CANADA

This was another one of those special charter trips that was put together by the travel company, an experimental trip planned and worked out using British Airways Concorde as our carrier, flying us from London to Toronto with accommodation in the Toronto Sheraton Hotel. It was only a short trip of just five days but as it only takes just over three hours to fly there on this aircraft it was worth doing especially as the asking price was a bargain. We quickly decided to give it a go and quick action was needed as the flight was sold out over that weekend of advertising.

Toronto is the largest city and economic capital of Canada with over 2.5 million residents. The city was established in 1793. UNESCO rated Toronto as one of the world's most diverse cities with 50% of the population born outside of Canada. It has a low crime rate, a high standard of living and is considered as one of the world's most liveable places.

Dominating Toronto's skyline is the C N Tower with a height of 1,815ft (550m) it has been one of the world's tallest freestanding structures since its completion in 1976. There are two visitor areas, the main deck level at 1082ft (330m) and the higher Sky Pod at 1,466ft (450m). The Sky Pod is one of the highest public observation decks in the world. On a clear day it is possible to see 75 miles (120 kilometres) away.

At 1,135 ft (349m) is the Horizons Cafe and at 1,151ft (354m) is the "360 Restaurant", a revolving tower restaurant which completes a full rotation every 72 minutes, allowing the diners a panoramic view of the town. It attracts more than two million visitors annually. In 1995, the C N Tower was declared one of the Seven Modern Wonders of the World by the American Society of Civil Engineers.

Toronto is a city of high-rise buildings having some 2,000 over 300ft (90m) in height, second only to New York.

Our supersonic flight across the Atlantic Ocean was special and spellbinding. There was one thing on this flight that had an eerie strangeness about it.

We had been served drinks by an air hostess with five-star looks, I had a tall flute of Champagne sitting on the fold down table in front of me. Suddenly the glass moved on its own accord and slid from the front of the table to the back, about nine inches or so. I stared with disbelief, what kind of magic is this, is there a ghost on board or what? Things do not move on their own, so there must be a reason. After a lot of thinking-time had passed, I reasoned out, the pilot must have moved it. I think the aircraft must have reached

NIAGARA FALLS

TORONTO

The boat named 'Maid of the Mist' is heading into the spray. The Mass of blue on the two decks is the hundreds of oilskin coated passengers.

Toronto's CN Tower.

maximum speed, on doing so the pilot would have switched off the engines afterburners, the sudden loss of their thrust would have slowed the aircraft down and us with it. However, my glass of Champagne, not being restrained, continued on at the same speed that it was going. I think it has something to do with Einstein's theory on time and space (I only think it has). I prefer this possibility to that of having a ghost on board.

(Afterburners provide short term extra thrust. This is achieved by injecting additional fuel into the jet engine downstream of the turbine area, this fuel is ignited by the hot exhaust gases which gives the advantage of significantly increased total engine thrust and therefore speed, the disadvantage is the high consumption of fuel. As a result they are only used for a limited time.)

On arrival at Toronto we quickly transferred to the Sheraton Hotel and soon found ourselves in the usual scene of Elizabeth unpacking and myself going through the Yellow Pages phone directory looking for suitable business contacts, ones we could call on during our short stay, or if too many, ones we could phone or write to after our return home. The following day armed with my list of companies, we toured the city in search of business.

Finding ourselves in this new city and getting from one place to another quickly by any means other than a taxi would be impossible, so taxis it was and during that first full day of hard work we flagged them down nine times in order to get them to take us to one after another of our chosen business contacts. Despite this intense day of travel to meeting our potential contacts all these were to prove, in the main, mostly negative. Just some possibility of business hovering in the wind.

So as there was only to be a few days here, it was now time for the adventure and pleasure side of our travel to take over.

The travel companies I use always supplied a complete package for their flying customers. That is the flight and the hotel, the food and drink, plus entertainment such as travelling to events and sightseeing, in this case, one of the events mid-week was a trip to the nearby Niagara Falls, this is a magnificent site straddling the USA and Canadian borders.

Niagara Falls is composed of two major sections that are divided by Goat Island, one is the Horseshoe Falls which is 2,600 ft (792 m) wide and are on the Canadian side of the border and the other named the American Falls are 1,060 ft (792 m) wide on the United States side. The falls have a height of 167 ft (52 m). When in full flow the volume of water reaches 200,000 cubic feet per second. It is the largest and most powerful waterfall in North America.

Naturally all this power is not wasted, upstream 60% of the Niagara River flow is diverted though four huge tunnels and then on through hydroelectric turbines to create and supply electric power to a large area of Canada and the USA. So as well as looking pretty the falls are pretty useful as well.

On arrival, we disembarked from our coaches at a nearby airfield, here we boarded in small groups the helicopters which were all fuelled up and standing there with their rotors rotating ready to take us up and through the thick mist and spray of these amazing falls. All helicopter flights are thrilling and all are different in the thrills they give. This one took off with a party of eight passengers on board and flew us up and down to view this awesome sight. The power and energy of Niagara is mind boggling, hovering in midair, pitched at a 45° angle and gazing down at this power, is fearsome. Like most things in life it was soon over and we had to return to our airfield base.

This however, was not to be the end of the day at the Falls, there was more to come. The next part of the day was where we joined in with the seeming madness of putting on blue oilskin water-proof clothing and boarding a boat called the Maid of the Mist along with hundreds of others which was to take us up to the very edge of the overwhelming powerful cascade of water (see picture).

After we recovered from the soaking, we returned to the hotel and found the rest of our stay was to be a tamer programme such as visiting the local market, the historic landmarks and such similar places.

We soon found that after many charming hours and days spent here, it was time to return home. We arrived at the airport only to be informed that our flight would be delayed for technical reasons, some two hours. This delay normally for air travellers is not too bad but two hours delay in the luxurious Concorde lounge at these airports is not good, it has its dangers. It can be a quite a strain on the best of us to fight off the constant offering of free fancy food, the fine wines and strong drinks which can in two hours weaken some of the strongest of us.

The blonde in the picture, after two hours of lounge pampering, is displaying the relaxed atmosphere of the passengers on board Concorde shortly after the take off.

Mid flight, the dinner was served (a sample of the menu is shown).

After our return home I considered the trip, on the business side it had limited possibility but contacts made can sometimes flourish in the future. So, a worthwhile journey plus the pleasure side which was full of thrills.

MENU

TORONTO - LONDON

APERITIFS - CHAMPAGNE

APPETIZERS
Canape Selection Including Smoked Salmon
Banquette of Caviar and Foie Grass Mousse with Apple

Fresh Nova Scotia Lobster Presented with Mango
and Papaya Relish

MAIN COURSES

Grilled Fillet of Beef with Wild Mushrooms, Shallots
and Parsley served with Grilled Tomato, French Beans
Carrots and Jettee Promenade Potatoes

OR

Bakes Fresh Salmon with Cracked Pepper, Tomato, Corn
and Coriander Salsa Garnished with Asparagus
Baby Carrots and Parsley Potatoes

OR

Steamed Breast of Chicken with Julienne or Root Vegetables
Moistened with a Butter and Herb Sauce Accompanied by
Pilaf Rice, Leaf Spinach and Patty Pans

SALAD BOWL

Mixed Seasonal Salad Served with Walnut Vinaigrette

DESSERT

Chocolate Tulip Filled with Sambucca Cream
and Cappuccina Mouse

ASSORTED CHEESE
A selection of English Stilton, Farmhouse Cheddar
and French Brie with Butter, Crackers and Crudites

COFFEE - TEA
Coffee, Decaffeinated Coffee or Tea
Swerved with selection of Friandises

BAR SERVICE

APERITIFS AND SPIRITS

A range of drinks from around the world to whet the
appetite - Sweet and Dry Vermouth, Campari, Medium Sherry,
John Walker's Oldest Scotch Whisky, Bourbon Rye
Tanqueray Gin, Bacardi Rum, Smirnoff Silver Label Vodka

COCKTAILS

Prepared to your choice from the range of Beverages
Carried on board.

SOFT DRINKS

A selection of traditional and modern soft drinks for
All Tastes - Aqua Libra, Fresh Orange Juice, Tomato Juice
Bitter Lemon, Tonic Water, Ginger Ale, Lemonade, Cola
Still or Sparkling Mineral Water

BEERS

Ale, Lager, Low Alcohol Lager

DIGESTIFS

An excellent selection of classic aged Digestifs and
Traditional Liqueurs for you to enjoy. 20 years old
Tawney Port, Cognac, Prunier XO. Tres Vielle Grande
Champagne, Drambuie, Cointreau, Bailey's Irish Cream
Tia Maria, Glenmorangie Single Highland Malt Whisky
Amaretto Di Saronno, Benedictine, Grand Marnier

CONCORDE TO AQABA

As we disembark the BBC TV film crew are there one step ahead of us to record our week in Jordan.

Chapter 10

CONCORDE TO THE KINGDOM OF JORDAN

This trip was the reverse of our usual business followed by pleasure travel planning. On this journey we were heading to Jordan in search of pleasure and adventure which was to prove more bountiful than any of our other world travels. We were aware, as this was not an English speaking country, the prospect of business for us would be limited, however, there would be a business world using English and the schools teach it as a second language. So although contacts would be difficult, there could be some opportunity to investigate.

This trip to Jordan was an extra special two for one last minute deal I had managed to negotiate and it proved to be a mind-blowing experience.

Jordan is a middle eastern country bordered by Iraq in the northeast, Syria in the north, Saudi Arabia in the southeast, Israel in the west and has a population of some six plus million. "So a pretty active part of the world to visit".

Our Supersonic Concorde flight at Mach 2 from London to Aqaba, a small coastal town situated on the shore of the Gulf of Aqaba, on the Red Sea coast of Jordan, only took 3 hours. During this time on board we were wined and dined in the superb Concorde fashion.

On arrival we disembarked and were led to a reception area where again fancy food and drink was laid out like a mini banquet, all offered to us by the King of Jordan, although not in need of such a treat, we all accepted their hospitality with pleasure. There is often great pride and excitement in many countries to have Concorde and its passengers visit them as guests and this royal feast was laid on proudly to welcome us to their land.

This trip had a slight difference to it. Apart from the overwhelming beauty and the many attractions of Jordan it had for us the extra drama of a BBC film crew who were there to record all of our days and events for the TV holiday programme "Wish You Were Here" and we were all to be a part of their filming.

Before I could consider looking out for business contacts, we were immediately thrown into a most fascinating week of one amazing day after another.

After leaving the airport, several coaches took all 100 of us out to a restored nineteenth century village called Taybet Zaman. This renovated hillside village of some 96 houses won the 1997 Global Tourism Award. At the presentation by Sir Colin Marshall and David Bellamy, the latter commented: "Some people recycle paper and

The restored village of Taybet Zaman a recycled 19th century settlement of 96 homes, shops, Turkish baths even a Ballroom plus the village square. The houses look crude to the eye but are built to stand against time and are cool and elegant on the inside.

ROSE RED CITY OF PETRA
Tourists walking through the "Siq", a long narrow fissure in the rocks that surround Petra and far right coming out of the long fissure to be mesmerised by the ancient Fortress City.

bottles, in Jordan they have recycled a complete village." This carefully converted place was to be our home-base for the first half of our week in Jordan.

Early the next day we were taken by coaches to nearby Petra. This is an amazing 2000 year old city which has been carved into the high cliffs of coloured rocks. Petra, often called the Rose Red City lies among the mountains which form the eastern flank of Arabah (Wadi Araba), the large biblical Valley of Jordan running from the Dead Sea to the Gulf of Aqaba. It is famous for the many homes and work rooms carved deeply into the high cliffs of multi-coloured rocks which surround the area. The entrance to the City is through a very high and long 1.25k narrow rock fissure called the Siq.

This long hidden site was revealed to the Western world by the brave Swiss explorer J. L. Burckhardt in 1812. Petra was first established around 600 BC by the Nabatean Arabs a nomadic tribe who settled in the safety of this enclosed area.

Petra only became accessible to Europeans when they were accompanied by local guides along with armed escorts after World War 1 around 1919.

Petra was designated as a UNESCO World Heritage Site in 1985 when it was described as "one of the most precious cultural properties of Man's heritage, one of the Wonders of the World."

After lunch we were off again in our coaches this time to a place I have longed to visit since I was a boy, Wadi Rum, known by some as the Moon on Earth, it is one of the world's most beautiful deserts. This is the area where the historic hero of the first world war, Lawrence of Arabia, mobilized the various Arab tribes into a strong fighting force that he led through the excessive heat and almost impregnable terrain of the Jordanian desert. Their mission was to attack from the rear and to overthrow the very powerful Turkish fort that overlooked and controlled the Red Sea at Aqaba. Fortunately, the big heavy guns at the fort were fixed to fire out to sea as an unexpected attack through this most fearsome desert was not thought feasible-how wrong they were.

Our day at Wadi Rum went well. There is not a lot you can do in the average desert, but given Wadi Rum, a desert full of mountains and hills and a four wheel drive jeep, things are different. We were soon driving off through the changing scenery and colours of the high craggy rocks, the deep valleys and sand dunes, all marvellous. However, most nice times can have some form of irritant. Often it is the menacing mosquito which can be the cause of distraction, for me in my most magical place my irritant was a doctor.

JORDAN DESERT - Wadi Rum

The Seven Pillars of Wisdom, so called by Lawrence of Arabia in 1917.

Getting ready to return, our convoy of jeeps started up and aimed for home just before the sun set and the black of the night was on us. They all revved up and the race was on across the dimly lit desert back to base. Lovely, gripping stuff, but suddenly my senses are being brought back to reality. I find myself listening to one of my travelling companions next to me. It was Doctor Boring bellowing in my ear on how he wondered if he was being missed back at home and he continued to keep telling me what a fine fellow he was for some long time. However, there were still a few miles to go so turning a deaf ear to the boring practitioner, who was completely oblivious to his marvellous surroundings of nature at its best. I managed to return my mind to the thrill of the race, only to be beaten and to come in with second place.

Our stay at Taybet Zamon, the charming restored village, had all the ingredients to hold the visitor spellbound from day to night. One such event was the Gala Dinner with all its finery and delightful range of exotic foods complete with the traditional sword swallowers and belly dancers but our stay here had come to an end as all things do and it was time to move on to Amman, the capital of Jordan.

Amman is a modern City with its hotels, shopping malls and centres, also the old is there with the Roman Amphitheatre and various Roman sites such as the famous city of Jerash, to many the best preserved example of a Roman city in the Middle East. Its paved streets are lined with hundreds of carved columns. The paving stones on the roads are rutted with the wear from thousands of Roman chariot wheels over many years. The massive Corinthean columns are there showing us the skills of those ancient craftsmen and stonemasons. A day spent here one can imagine a trip back 2,000 years into Roman times.

For us to get to Amman our Concorde had stayed with us on stand-by for the week and had been parked in Aqaba Airport, whilst the air crew, and the aircraft "Flying" ground crew technician had joined all of us in the hotels for the week's stay as well.

Our flight from Aqaba to Amman was Subsonic due to the short flying distance. Here again the pride of having this aircraft visit their air space, caused the air traffic controller to give us straight through air clearance to land at Amman Airport much to the delight of the waiting TV camera crews and reporters. After disembarking we were taken to the modern Marriott Hotel for a comfortable stay of a few days. From our new base we could explore some of the other great wonders of Jordan.

Various trips to Roman sites such as the town's amphitheatre were laid on but then a trip, strangely different to any others, was a journey to the Dead Sea

THE DEAD SEA

In the west of Jordan there lies the world's lowest land mass and water body - the Jordan Valley and the Dead Sea. To the left the BBQ on the shores of the sea all are jolly and waiting for their food and drink To the right the same BBQ with abandoned tables, defeated by a million flies but not for long, after the lights went out, all was to be well.

which is 1,316 feet (402 meters) below sea level, the lowest place on earth where people live, Having flown here at 60,000 feet above sea level, the highest any airline passengers have ever flown above the surface of the earth, we were now swimming 1,316ft below the earths sea level. The Dead Sea area is a strange world, you can feel it in the air and if you go for a swim into the sea it contains so much salt and minerals you just float on top of the water.

It was in the evening when the best was to come. On the shores of the sea a superb sunset barbecue had been set out for us. In the distance several miles across the water were the lights of the towns of Jerusalem and Bethlehem both silhouetted by the setting sun slowly sinking behind the hills. As the food and drink began to arrive we were shocked to see a large number of others were joining us. No, not the local yobbo's, it was worse than that - it was a giant fly attack, millions of the little critters. The food was quickly covered and removed and then the killing started but we were heavily outnumbered. Despite our efforts their numbers were about to defeat us when some passivist in the crowd cried: "Put all of the lights off for a while," which was duly done. Fifteen minutes later it was on with the lights and unbelievably not one fly in sight and they were not to return during the whole of our evening.

So it was on with the BBQ along with the music and entertainment and all went well for a great evening. Travelling in Jordan had been full of wonder and excitement but there was more to come.

The next day was an early start and it was to be a day to strain the brain. We were taken to the Al-Mahatta Station for a train ride into the middle of the Jordan desert to visit the old Turkish Fort of Dabaa - but getting there was to be different. First the journey by train was unique, we were to travel in the actual train used by Lawrence of Arabia in his fight against the Turks in 1917, and his victory ride into Damascus to announce their capture of the powerful coastal fort of Aqaba.

This steam-hauled vintage train puffing its thick black smoke took all of us out through the outskirts of Amman into the hot dry sands of the sun-seared desert whilst roving musicians and entertainers walked amongst us. After an hour or so the train began to slow down, glancing out of the window we could see why, a dozen or more fierce-looking men on horseback were attacking our train and they began firing guns. The train eventually stopped and we were boarded by some of these men, a young lady standing near me on the end of our carriage outside footplate was grabbed and taken hostage. (see picture). She was taken onto the leader's horse and they galloped away out of sight. I was slow to react, I should have leapt forward and

A VINTAGE STEAM TRAIN HAULING FIVE COACHES

Leaving the outskirts of the capital Amman and heading for the desert fort of Dabaa.

ATTACK ON OUR TRAIN TO DABAA FORT

As we journeyed to the Fort, our train began to slow down. Glancing out of the window we could see why - a dozen or more fierce looking men on horseback appeared at full gallop from behind a sand dune and were attacking our train, some firing guns. The train was finally brought to a halt and a young woman was taken hostage from among us.

After an hour or so the train began to slow down as a dozen or more men on horseback attacked our train and began firing rifles. The train stopped and a hostage was taken from us. The fair haired lady in the picture was pulled from the platform at the rear of our rail coach and onto the lap of the man on horseback where she was taken away at a brisk gallop. I just had time to grab this action photo of the scene then slowly it dawned on us and we all realised it was a theatrical stunt put on to excite us - and it did. We quickly relayed the good news to two old ladies further down our rail coach where they were close to fainting.

knocked old long nose of his horse and tried to save the "maiden in distress." However, the photographer in me overwhelmed the hero instinct and the picture was snatched instead. It was just as well I was too slow to knock old long nose of his horse as it turned out to be a surprise theatrical stunt put together to excite us, and guess what? It did. We quickly relayed the good news to the two old ladies further down our carriage where they were close to fainting.

The train pulled forward slowly for another half a mile then came to a halt along side a range of Bedhouin tents where food and drink was laid out for us as a refresher. Our hotel mobil kitchen staff had taken out a supply of goods to keep us happy on route but more than that they sent out a grand piano and bow tie pianist where in the middle of this vast desert he embraced us with the soft music of Mozart and the Lawrence of Arabia film theme music, all very elegant and a nice touch for dining even in the desert.

After taking our refreshment, the train's whistle blew and it was time to leave and move on to the Fort. I was so busy talking to the men on horseback that I missed the call, the next thing I was aware of was that the train was on the move and I was a long way from it. My sprint had an Olympic quality about it and I just managed to grab the last handrail and drag myself aboard. The horsemen were looking a bit too tough for me to want to get to know any further, or any longer, so I was relieved to make the train. All during the trip the TV crew had been busily filming so we were all on our best behaviour. The train chugged on along this single line track for another hour or so and finally stopped. We all climbed down and started off walking the long trek through the sand and rocks and under a fierce sun to the desert fort, which we could just make out several miles in the distance.

An elegant lunch was set up for us in this unique place again by the hotel's mobile kitchen crew. Towards the end of this elegant desert dining, the gates of this old fort suddenly opened with a creaking sound and before us were the King's Pipers of the Royal Jordanian Army, who marched out and proceeded to entertain us with their music which added one more delight to the day.

After our return to the hotel and later that evening, another "not to know what to expect" surprise was laid on by the tour operator. This travel company always arranged a secret event.

We had been asked to dress our best for this special event and were taken by coaches to one of the city of Amman's high hilltops. Here there are the remains of the Roman Temple of Hercules, the strong man of their Gods.

A WALK IN THE DESERT

Our train billowing black smoke in the distance and there is a lot further to go for the scattered 100 who are making their way on foot to the Fort. A long trek on a difficult surface.

From this high position we found ourselves looking down on to the lights and lives of the town's people below us, and looking up we see the sparkling beautiful star-laden night sky.

We sat down to a five star meal with music from a famous female pianist floating through the crisp clear air to enchant us as we all became totally absorbed by the scene, picturing the past diners, such as those tough toga clad Romans and their elegant dressed women, who would have been dining here in the same spot very much like us, but some 2,000 years before us.

The following day was the time to head for home. The incredible faster than sound supersonic flight went well, and the week's magic was consigned to memory, however it was a memory so intense and so deep that it was to take us six months to get it to lose its constant hold.

DESERT DINING

Our trek to the Fort was met by an elegant lunch laid out by the Hotel's mobile kitchen staff and further enhanced by the King of Jordan's Royal Band of Pipers.

A TOAST FROM THE TRAVELLER

Dennis and Elizabeth at the Fort wishing you the reader, All The Best.

Chapter 11
CONCORDE TO THE USA
NEW YORK AND ANTIQUE
TYPEWRITERS

This is not a place that would be requiring my reconditioned manual typewriters in any way whatsoever, I was well aware of the fact that my usual type of export market was not here. However, I had for some time considered the possibility of supplying antique typewriters to the numerous New York Antique shops and dealers. So, with these thoughts in mind and the appearance of a possible two-for-one flight, which I managed to acquire we set about going there to sound out the market.

One of the travel companies I study and use had a transatlantic flight by Concorde coupled with a one week's stay in the famous New York Plaza Hotel coming up soon. I managed to book, at short notice, two seats on a special two-for-one deal. The luxury and rarity of a trip such as this is understandably, expensive when it is compared to sub-sonic air travel and a less famous accommodation.

This travel company was running a Charter trip using a B.A Concorde to fly us there as opposed to the expensive normal daily Concorde from London to- New York service run by British Airways. This meant, as a charter trip, the price worked out to be about half of the cost of a normal BA Concorde scheduled service.

An even better price for us was the chance of a two-for-one offer, which resulted in us paying half the charter price, it was a very good value trip and now it was even better.

Two days before the journey was to be made we had a telephone call from the travel company explaining that our Concorde had been pulled out of service for urgent technical maintenance work. This meant no aircraft, no travel as all the other Concordes would be in use. However, British Airways quickly assessed the situation and calculated that the 100 passengers on our charter flight could be absorbed in their daily scheduled Concorde service. They proposed, as there were vacancies available, to take a third of our group of passengers half a day earlier, another third would travel close to our original travel time and the remaining third half a day late. We were offered the last option the half day late Concorde but to compensate for our few hours of lost time, we were offered an exceedingly generous £500 each financial rebate from British Airways. By now, what with it being a special-priced charter trip, plus our last minute two-for

CONCORDE COCKPIT
This shows the British Airways air crew plus an extra person in the jump seat. Some of these chartered flights carried this extra person who would give an hours commentary over the intercom of the design and the technology that made this aircraft so different from all the others.

one-deal, and now on top of that, their was British Airways generous reimbursement, by now we were down to paying a fraction of the price that my fellow travellers had paid. To fly in the world's most magnificent aircraft and to stay in the luxury one of the world's most famous hotels at such a reduced price was almost making me feel like a crook, however I quickly convinced myself to shake off these negative thoughts. We were, after all, helping out by taking those empty places!

New York City is one of the global economic centres with its business, financial, legal and media organizations having worldwide influence. It is also the home of the United Nations.

Over 20 million tourists come to New York City each year visiting the Empire state building, Ellis Island, Broadway's 39 theatres, the Museums and other attractions such as Central Park, Times Square, the Bronx Zoo and there are numerous fancy shops along Madison and Fifth Avenues to visit.

Weather-wise New York has a humid climate. The winters can be cold, the spring and autumn are unpredictable ranging from cold and snowy to hot and humid, summers are sometimes warm and humid with temperatures of 90°F or higher. So the weather it would seem is as busy as its town people.

I have a customer who is an American citizen. He owns and runs a company in Croydon, south of London. We have supplied and maintained his IBM typewriters for some years. On a recent visit to our showroom he gave me a newspaper containing a story about a New York typewriter shop similar to ours. In the article the business owner described some of their sales markets which included supplying antique typewriters to authors, some very well known who preferred to write their stories on old traditional manual machines. They also supply to antique typewriter collectors. These people are growing in number and include some well known names, one being the Hollywood actor Tom Hanks who has a collection of some 80 antique typewriters. After reading this article I put their company on my intended visiting list.

On arrival in New York we booked in to the Plaza Hotel. It was built in the same era as the Ritz in London, one of those old fashioned hotels that was built to provide grace and grandeur to the visitor, along with its marvellous fixtures and features and customs. Its location was right next to Central Park, one of the largest and well known open areas in the crowded city. From this position it was easy to target our proposed potential business contacts. The hotel was much like most hotels in that it comprises of numerous rooms and numerous people rushing to and fro.

THE PLAZA HOTEL NEW YORK

Horse drawn carrages ready to take visiters around Central Park

The Plaza, one of America's most celebrated hotels, opened its doors in October 1907 amid reports describing it as 'the greatest hotel in the world'. Kings, Presidents, Ambassadors, stars of stage, screen and sports, as well as business executives and visitors from all parts of the world have gathered and stayed at The Plaza. Located at Fifth Avenue and Central Park South,. Its four restaurants cater to the many different tastes and moods of its sophisitcated cliente'le . The Palm Court, located amid a profusion of greenery, is a New York institution. The Oak Bar, New Yorks' most famous watering hole, serves drinks to leading New York celebrities and visitors. The Oyster Bar recalls the warmth of an English Pub, whilst The Oak Room is reminiscent of an exclusive mens club. Ceilings, 24 feet high, dominate the room, sable oak walls with fluted columns and turn-of-the-century murals add refinement and elegance.

This one is different for New York because of its age, classical style and history. It has drawn in many celebrities over the years. One of the world reported events was the marriage of Michael Douglas to Catherine Zeta Jones, both from the acting and film world. This duo has thrilled and entertained millions of us with their skills and role plays for many years. Their wedding must have been a special sight to see. Unfortunately we were not there at the time but whilst we were there we managed to observe a number of well known faces walking around the lobby and seated in the dining rooms. Talking about dining, there is a point to remember with New York: the portions are often large and somewhat different to other countries size values. Here is an example.

One day Elizabeth and I decided to take our evening dinner in the hotel's famous Oak Room restaurant. After examining the menu for some time, the waiter came to take our order. Elizabeth chose an excellent rack of lamb. I being a lover of crustations, chose the lobster. Now here is a point on size: the menu showed a 1½lb lobster at say x dollars and a 2½lb one at say xx dollars. The waiter appeared to be tired, worn out or just fed up with his job. His attempts to understand my London accent was straining him to his limit. After many attempts to explain our needs, I ended up just pointing at the menu and saying "Lobster Big One" meaning the larger 2½lb size one. This, of course, is more than any one person would sensibly need by far. However, somewhere unbeknown to me, on the outside menu board it had a special offer which said "Try the Big One" a 4lb lobster. The waiter eventually grunted and off he went. After the appropriate time, our meal was served all the trimmings and drinks turned up and then this monster arrived. Apparently I had triggered the cooking of this magnificent creature. Before me was an enormous 4lb lobster. I looked at its size in disbelief and said: "The poor creature was probably 30 or 40 years old and in its prime". The urge to become a vegetarian dawned upon me. I felt as though I was about to eat the kitchen pet.

In fact many restaurants keep lobsters fresh in tanks and they are only cooked when orders are taken. I said to Elizabeth "I can't believe this". Then jokingly I said "this beautiful creature might have been in their tank for years and now the staff are probably saying to each other, "What bad luck, she has escaped the pot for all these years with us and now some damn Limey has just ordered her. Poor old Lucky our pet lobster." I could imagine weeping and disbelief as they saw their longtime friend being executed to satisfy me this foreign fiend.

However the dining went well and I was relieved to see we did not achieve mental breakdown of the kitchen staff on the loss of their longterm friend. I shuddered at the sight of the final bill for the meal. I realised I must sharpen my wits and find the secret of obtaining half-price lobsters to go with halfprice travel.

The following afternoon whilst strolling around the city a light shower passed overhead so we dived into the nearby Sheraton Hotel where I knew of a cosy cocktail bar that also offered a pleasant view to watch the world go by. The shower soon passed as did the first cocktail. I decided to extend our stay in the bar with fresh drinks. We then became aware of a large number of heavily armed police. They appeared to be swarming inside and outside the hotel. We soon found out, that apparently the U.S. President was due within the next hour to hold a special meeting in the hotel's facility rooms and so security was on high alert.

These secure rooms on the top floor are reached by a special lift that takes the presidential car and it's occupants, from the road, straight up to the right floor where they can walk through to the conference table.

A short time later, we decided to leave the cocktail bar and return to our hotel. As we walked down the main road we noticed all the approach side roads were being barricaded off. No one was allowed to cross the main road, therefore, within minutes a large number of people were amassed four or five deep on these barricades which stretched for half a mile or so. As we walked, on, the President's procession appeared, first there were the motorcycle escorts, then security cars galore and in the middle of the procession was the President doing the customary hand waving to the crowd. He was probably thinking: "This is a fine turn out to see me," but in fact, nobody we met on the barriers had any idea why they were being held up. It seems that any Government anywhere can look impressively popular with the aid of half a mile of barriers.

My search for suitable antique dealers, who might have made possible my idea of exporting old and antique typewriters to the New York market, proved to be a failed project. However, I had one more very special business contact to meet and I planned to call on them on the Saturday morning. The company was the one mentioned in the press article my American customer gave me back in our typewriter shop in England. I looked up their address in the Yellow Pages, made a note of it together with their telephone number and was ready to visit them. I had not made a proper business appointment, I was relying merely on calling in to see them as and when it suited us. Well, it was 10 o'clock on Saturday morning and the time to call on them now suited us. I also knew they were open until 1 p.m. on Saturdays so off we set. According to the address taken from Yellow Pages, it was only half an hour's walk to their typewriter shop and we had three hours to get there. On arrival at the address it turned out to be a completely different type of business operating from there, so I figured I must have written down the wrong premises number. Therefore, assuming the road name was correct, all we had to do was walk up and down the road and we would find the right establishment. I did not realise how long this road was to be, but after exploring its length from end to end I realised either the Yellow Pages had printed the wrong address or more likely I had written the wrong one down. Whatever, we were in the wrong place and time was running out.

I had not bought my mobile phone with me however, we eventually found a public telephone, I dialled the telephone number I had recorded and sure enough someone in the typewriter shop replied. I asked for their address and then looked it up on our map only to discover we were a long way from them. The time now was over two hours since leaving the hotel. In fact we had only about thirty minutes before the shop was due to close. Taking all the short cuts we could at last saw our goal. We finally stood at a large set of traffic lights facing this New York business, the, typewriter shop we had come so far to see.

The heavy traffic and the long hold-up on the lights was the final straw. As we stood waiting we saw all the staff emerge from the building pull down the shutters, lock the door and walk off. The traffic lights finely changed but by the time we had crossed the road all sight of the staff had gone. We had flown across the Atlantic Ocean, over 3,000 miles in just over 3 hours, only to miss my number one New York business possibility by 30 seconds. Well, that is what comes from my very careless planning. Our trip was to end the next day so a further call on them was not possible. Personal contact is essential in what I was planning. So I said, concealing my anger at being so careless; Perhaps another day--and to our surprise a year later that day came.

Chapter 12

LONDON to NEW YORK
CONCORDE to PARIS

It was just over a year since our first New York trip when I spotted another special offer. This time one of the travel companies I use had put together a nice sounding week. It was a one-off trial run where the travel company reserved 40 seats on an Air France Concorde flying from New York USA to Paris, France. The idea was we would be flown by British Airways Boeing 747 jumbo from London to New York where we would stay in the Sheraton Hotel in Manhattan for four nights. We would then fly Air France Concorde to Paris for a further three nights staying in the Hilton Hotel and then finally flying British Airways back to London. A good sounding trip and all at a bargain price when one considers what is being offered which also included entertainment such as a tour of New York by coach and also a tour of New York in the air by helicopter plus a night at the theatre on Broadway, plus similar events when we were in Paris.

After our arrival in New York one of the first things I arranged was a business meeting with the typewriter company I missed by thirty seconds the last time we were here. Our meeting was successful, and from that I was also introduced to several other in town businesses that were in the antique trade. These we have since supplied with a large number of the rarer makes of Antique typewriters that are more easily found in the U.K and which are scarcer in the USA.

On the pleasure side of the trip a coach journey was arranged to take us on a half day, sightseeing tour of the town stopping here and there doing the things tourists do, which took us through the morning. The rest of the day was spent by combing stores such as Bloomingdales, Maceys, and Tiffany, with Elizabeth searching for bargain buys.

Next day we were taken to the Heliport where we loaded up and took to the sky. Our flight took us all around New York and the famous Twin Towers, now so tragically lost, a loss that was felt and suffered worldwide. Then onto other sights and during our return to the heliport we flew around Ellis Island and looked down on to the giant French gift to the USA, the Statue of Liberty.

Back on the ground we decided to make our way to the highest building in town the Twin Towers, correctly titled the World Trade Centre. Tourists loved to visit the top floor of this, one of the world's tallest building where they could dine, shop, or just view the tiny world beneath them. As we took the lift we noticed that they went so fast the

New York Harbour, our helicopter is ready to take us on a tour of the town where we flew around the twin towers and out over Ellis Island with its Giant Statue of Liberty.

floor indicator was counting in tens. I recall standing on the top floor in one particular glass observation spot where you could look straight down to the street below. There seemed to be an ant-sized world in motion which is not all that surprising after all we were over 100 floors high.

The World Trade Centre was a wonderful modern complex of seven buildings in Lower Manhattan. The complex, located in the heart of New York City's downtown financial district, contained 13.4 million square feet of office space. Drama had struck the buildings before with a serious fire in 1975 in the North Tower which spread throughout the 11th floor, and a terrorist bombing in 1993, when a truck loaded with 1500 lbs of explosives was detonated in the underground car park leaving a 100ft hole through five levels of concrete.

Six people died over 100 injured and 50,000 other workers and tourists were trapped full of fear and gasping for air as the smoke and thick dust rose up through the floors. With the electric power cut and the lifts knocked out thousands were forced to walk down darkened stairwells, some taking over two, trembling hours to reach safety. A horrible scene but this did not deter those strong-willed workers and other visitors from returning to the towers.

As the world knows, another attack was made on September 11, 2001. Nearly 3,000 people died and the buildings in the complex were destroyed by two suicide flown jet airliner. The two tall towers No 1 and 2 collapsed causing a domino effect as they fell crushing building No 3 and damaging beyond repair building's 4, 5, and 6. These were later demolished and the site cleared. On March 13, 2006 site engineers arrived at the World Trade Centre to start surveying. This marked the official start of re-construction.

After two more superb days of sightseeing, shopping and seeking business, we were due to start the second part of this three legged journey.

The next day it was off to the airport for our Air France Concorde flight to Paris, 3,500 miles away but only just over 3 hours to get there in this French Queen of the sky.

The picture taken through the lobby window of the departure lounge inside the airport building shows the aircraft being prepared for departure and seemingly artistically highlighted by the reflection of the lighting, making this a unique Concorde photograph. The flight across the Atlantic Ocean was as good as flying gets, the speed over 1400 mph and 60,000ft high. The in-flight dining had a French influence to the three courses provided, plus the wine waiter offering his superb selection of vintage wines and champagnes, and after consuming the fine food it was followed by a range of fine

Air France Concorde and reflection of strip lighting on the Airport's windows, creating a unique picture, seemingly intended to highlight the Queen of the Sky.

vintage digestives such as 20 year old port wines and rare old brandies and all this served on Damask table linen along with the finest Royal Doulton table china.

This would have been classed as excellent fine dining in any restaurant anywhere, but here for us it was very easy to forget we were 10 miles high in the Sky.

I recall talking to a young member of the Air France cabin staff who was very proud to be part of this supersonic way of flying. He told me proudly that our initial acceleration would be faster than a sports Porsche car, 0-60mph in four seconds and that is not on full power due to the noise limitations restrictions here, he quoted. Meanwhile, I just hoped those engine bolts were tight.

A year later in France this aircraft crashed in flames upon take-off killing all the 109 passengers and crew on board.

The reason for the disaster started when Concorde on its take off, ran over a small strip of metal that had fallen from a previous aircraft, this cut into one of its high pressure tyres causing it to explode hurling off large pieces of rubber tyre that hit the under wing, this resulted in a shock wave rupturing the wings internal fuel tank. The leaking fuel ignited setting the aircraft on fire. Despite the pilots' efforts to maintain control as they tried to seek out a nearby landing strip all was lost, the fire took a stronger hold and within two minutes caused this marvellous aircraft to crash in flames and all on board perished as well as a number of people on the ground.

This disaster took its toll even wider. The British and French looked into making the aircraft safer, new stronger tyres were ordered and the wings fuel tanks were lined inside with re-enforcing neoprene panels.

British Airways, after spending millions of pounds strengthening the fuel tanks, put their Concorde fleet back into service on the lucrative Atlantic Ocean crossing flying London to New York. However, despite a good press, a large number of the regular wealthy people that flew this way had lost their confidence in the aircraft after seeing the dramatic film coverage of the French plane on fire trying desperately to take off and then when it did, within seconds, seeing it fall back to the ground and explode.

What most of these people would not know was that when they were flying at this extreme height of 60,000 ft, it had its dangers, if the cabin air pressure system suddenly failed all the people in the aircraft would implode and be off to a" better place" within two seconds. As they say what you don't know you don't worry about.

With the fall of their regular supersonic passengers British Airways eventually decided it was no longer economical to keep their fleet of six Concordes in service. And so, because of that sad day in France and that one small metal

THE EIFFEL TOWER

Built in 1887 as an observation and radio broadcast tower by the architect Gustave Eiffel, it is the tallest structure in Paris, 1063 ft (319M) tall and one of the most recognized monuments in the world and one of the most visited with over 6 million visitors a year and more than 200,000,000 since its construction. Not everyone loves the tower, one man, novelist Guy de Madpassant, hated the tower but ate lunch every day in its restaurant. When asked why he answered "it is the only place in Paris where you could not see the damn thing". During WW2 and the retreat of the German Troops from Paris, Hitler ordered it to be demolished but General Dietrick Von Chaltity disobeyed the order as he did not want to go down in history as the man who destroyed the Eiffel Tower.

strip on the runway, the flying days of this, the most magnificent airliner ever built, the Queen of the Sky, were over and the world lost its most beautiful flying machine.

After landing in Paris, France, we were taken to the Hilton Hotel for our stay. I knew the chance of finding business contacts here would be zero because of their use of a different keyboard layout and even in their ex-colonies in Africa they would be using the French keyboard. So it was just to be a few days of leisure and pleasure. Here again our tour company arranged for the usual half day tour of the city plus a visit to and up the Eiffel Tower, and in the evening taking the traditional casual walk along the banks of the River Seine. Here one can absorb the late hour, with the sights and sounds of the scene drawing us in. The succulent smells of the snacks coming from vendors cooking food to sell from their mobile stalls, whilst gently, almost silently along side all of us, the glistening river flowed on its way.

After much wining, dining and general sightseeing, it was time to head for home. Our British Airways flight brought us back to London to start another week of "Life in the Typewriter Shop."

Travelling over many years to obtain our oversea's export typewriter sales and coupling it with pleasure and adventure activity, proved to be worthwhile, both in the foreign sales orders we achieved, and also from the many exciting places visited, plus exotic high quality supersonic travel high in the sky.

However, obtaining older style manual typewriters for these foreign markets in sufficient number was difficult, as the machines drastically dwindled from the 10 million that had become available to the now hard to find few.

This Typing Machine, so called gold rush, had been bled dry and was nearly over.

After 15 years this re-homing of millions of our country's redundant writing machines "this vein of gold " was all but exhausted, and has now, for us, sadly come to an end.

It had been a very exciting and interesting time for those of us involved. In our case it drew us out of the shop, as we travelled the world seeking business and adventure.

It is pleasing and very rewarding to know that our reconditioned typewriters are now being used in over 50 countries worldwide.

Our next chapter is very much removed from exciting travel. It is back to our home base "The Shop", where we recall 50 tales of encounters with the nice and the nasty, the sometimes difficult and often unusual customers. Not so exciting as world travelling but pretty tense at times. It is real "Life in the Typewriter Shop" for us to deal with.

Chapter 13

50 Tales from the Typewriter Shop

Sometimes I feel we are like a couple of goldfish. We have spent the best part of a long time gazing out of this our special bowl. Day after day, year after year we work away, constantly glancing up as any outside movement draws our attention.

The goldfish bowl is of course our shop, and the only view to the outside world is through a pane of glass some twenty feet wide and ten feet high, here we see time pass by.

For over 35 years we have watched kids become mums, mums become grannies, boys become men and men become old boys. As the years have ticked by we see an endless change of faces on the young mothers as they deliver and collect their infants from the nursery school nearby.

Occasionally, I play a little joke on the infants as they head for their school. Amongst my collection of typewriters is a toy version which, when it is plugged into the electricity supply it plays a tune, the carriage moves from side to side as the keys strike the paper. Placed all over it are small comical mice which bob up and down and spin round and round. When the little kids stop to look in the window I switch it on from an electric socket some distance away. The kids love it and shout for Mum to come and have a look.

"Mum, the mice are dancing."

Well, as Mum comes to look, I switch off.

"No they are not," and Mum walks away.

The kid looks back and I switch on.

"Yes they are," the kid shouts. "Come and have a look."

Mum reluctantly comes back, but the funny thing is, it is switched off again and all is still. It is not long before the kids are moved on, looking somewhat puzzled

Right, back to looking through the window. We sit and work here six days a week and watch this part of the world go by. There are the regular long-term unemployed; off to the pub when it opens at eleven for a couple of pints, then into the betting shop next door for a couple of hours, mid-afternoon it's probably back home for a nap for another couple of hours, day after day, year after year.

I have already explained our shop location, but I will run through it again. Ours is one in a small parade of shops situated alongside traffic lights on a main trunk road leading into London. We are first in the parade then next door is a double-fronted car showroom followed by a kebab shop, an Indian takeaway, a ladies hairdressers, a betting shop, another double-fronted car showroom and lastly an all-day breakfast cafe. The whole parade has flats above, one of which is a knocking shop. Finally there is the Gander a detached pub on the corner. So, we are a parade that caters for all needs.

I find the knocking shop intriguing to watch. It is all very discreet. Work does not start until eleven in the morning, so it is not uncommon to see the odd desperate client pacing up and down. I remember one chap - who obviously did not want to be recognise walk past our window heading to the flat wearing a motorcycle helmet, but no motorcycle to be seen!

Another occasion I had a customer in my shop enquiring about fax machines, a little while later, I saw the same man ringing the bell on the knocking shop door. I think the trip to my shop was his means of covering his tracks with a false trail!

Most of the girls were quite attractive and all seemed happy with their lot. However I recall one who was pretty big and very powerful looking, dressed in her fancy, leopard skin, skin-tight, tights. It would have been a tough fellow to stand his ground and not do a runner when she answered the door.

The main road by which we are situated is a four lane, two each way trunk road, very busy and of course a blackspot for accidents with frequent minor car collisions but it has been the pedestrians who have suffered the most with quite a few deaths and casualties over the years. Ambulances and the medical helicopter have attended the scene with the wide road providing suitable access for a helicopter to land and do what it has to do.

As I said earlier, when we are in our goldfish bowl with glass so thick that very little noise penetrates we watch an almost silent moving picture: the countless times we see people walk into and bounce off the new, no-parking signpost erected by the local council.

You can imagine that over the years, with customer contacts numbering over a quarter of a million, we have come across many different types of character.

Customers have been as young as four to those who have reached their late nineties. We have a worldwide clientele different nationalities with many different customs. We have experienced the bright - cheerful - clever - brilliant - charming - lovely - friendly - aggressive - liars - cunning - thieving - smelly - difficult - dim and dreadful, they have been fat, thin, tall, short, all ages, all sizes. We try and love them all, the men, women, even the baby in the pram.We believe that if they have taken the time and trouble to visit us, then it is our job to do all we can to make their trip worthwhile.

So here we go, I have plucked from memory a variety of

some 50 Tales which have remained in our minds.

1) Customers are not always what they seem to be - we have had our share of thieves and villains, bouncing cheques and stolen cheques, not all that common, but they come along from time to time. The bouncing cheques add insult to injury, as the bank charge us an extra fee to return the dud back to us.

Before chip and pin arrived I remember an incident whereupon a stolen credit card was used to purchase a small typewriter for fifty pounds, which was the limit of guaranteed cover. However, the credit card company refused to honour it saying the signature did not match. I had to inform them, somewhat bluntly, that to my eye they did match, so the company did finally pay up.

One example of theft was executed by two men, they would look around at the various machines on display and while one distracts the sales staff, the other is helping himself to a small pocket size dictation machine or a laptop size printer both of which are easy to hide.

Another time we had a hold-up. I was on my own when, suddenly, six youths marched in through the front door. Two six-footers sandwiched me either side by pressing tightly against my shoulders, while the other four looked around to see what could be had. Suddenly, at some sort of signal, they all turned around and were off.

Smashing the front door and crawling through the broken glass for a quick steal was the habit of one man, usually about five-thirty in the morning. The clues he left behind were enough for me to work out that it was someone I knew well, someone on bad times, so I did not reveal my suspicions.

2) A husband and wife were looking to buy a new typewriter; they needed to phone home and ask their daughter the certain specifications required:

"Can I borrow your phone?" the wife asked.

"Of course," I replied. "Use this cordless one".

I dialled the number she gave me and handed it to her.

"It's not ringing," she said.

I listened. "Yes it is," I said.

She tried again. "No it isn't," she said.

Her husband joins in and listens. "Yes it is," he said.

She listens again and said angrily "It's not ringing."

"Hold on," her husband said. "Don't forget you are deaf in one ear."

"Yes," she said. "But that is the other ear."

The phone went on its rounds again, two or three more times, when she suddenly realises it was her, she has been listening for the ringing tone with the deaf ear. We all found it most amusing at the time.

3) A man down on his luck came into the shop recently and asked me to mend his watch.

"The watch repair shop wants three pounds to change the battery," he said. "I've got a spare one. Would you change it for me? I'll give you fifty pence if you do."

This I would be only too pleased to do, but I was suffering from the smell he was giving off.

I had to act pretty sharp before the paint peeled off the woodwork, so I made out that I did not have the tools to undo the watch. Holding my breath, I said."I can't, but tell you what, it will be easier and quicker if I give you the three pounds so the watch repairer can help you." Feeling quite safisfied by my own generosity, I delved into my pocket for the change and handed it to the chap.

"I don't want your charity - stick it." he said.

He slammed the door and was off.

4) A man brought his electronic typewriter in for service and repair: "Something wrong with the keyboard," he said.

"I will book it in and sort it out for you," I told him.

The machine goes off to the workshop where we discover that a liquid had been spilt into the keyboard. So we set about doing what has to be done and the machine was soon back in working order.

The customer called the next day to pick his typewriter up. "What was wrong?" he asked.

"Well someone has spilt some liquid into the keyboard, but it is up and running now," I replied. A puzzled look came on his face.

"I know what that must be - it's my damned cat, he's going barmy, he keeps going round peeing on everything, it's no good he will have to go, he's in for the chop."

5) Our mechanic collected a typewriter from a stationery shop we often dealt with and brought it in for repair. The job was done; the customer notified, and then they asked could we return it to their club office.

The machine was duly delivered to the office by the mechanic, but upon arrival he was surprised to be in a Sussex Nudist Camp. It was with great embarrassment that he carried the machine into the office. Further embarrassment followed for the poor young fellow as he made two subsequent trips to rectify more faults.

He reckoned though, that some of the elder campers would benefit from a quick run over with a steam iron.

6) We had an American chap and his wife who would often come in for a repair to their machine. Nice couple,

gracefully aging. The four of us were in close proximity sorting out the problem when the husband suddenly puts his hands on his chest and starts singing their national anthem from start to finish, very loud and about two feet from my ear. Kind of put me off track for a while. Well, I wasn't sure whether to clap or give him a tip, so I did neither, and got on with the problem at hand. The repair was soon done and they went away as happy as Larry, gladly before he started up again.

7) An expensive typewriter was in for repair some time back. The machine was an Adler Golf Ball, the very latest technology in those days. The repair was completed and I returned it to the company.

"Take it into that office, please," someone said. As I walked in the boss looked up and said: "Ah, good, we are very pleased to see that back that's our best one". Unfortunately, as he finshed talking and I walked forward, the handle of the door went neatly up my jacket sleeve. Well, when this sort of caper happens I and the machine go forward but my right arm stays with the door handle. Bang! Crash! The machine hits the floor and I write off a five hundred pound machine.

It follows on that dropped machines are bad news. Many a time we have customers come in saying they had dropped it down the stairs or was moving it only to be tripped up by the dog, or the kids had knocked it off the table. Often they cannot be repaired or the cost is uneconomically high. All the worse if it has been borrowed, many a friendship has come to an end this way.

8) There was the woman who brought back a manual typeriter which her husband had bought from us a few days previously:

"The machine's no good," she said angrily.

"What's the problem?" I politely asked.

"Well, it's the T and the H, they are the wrong way round. When my husband types THE, he gets HTE."

"Well, it's not the machine. It's your husband's typing," I replied.

"NO IT'S NOT," she shouted. "There is nothing wrong with his typing".

I showed her that when I struck the T key, it actually printed a T on the paper. But that was not good enough for her - her husband could not be wrong. Realising I was fighting a losing battle with another loony I agreed to take HTE machine back.

9) The picture shows the type basket of an Olympia manual typewriter. It was brought into the shop for a

The Officers typewriter, showing the black ribbon slightly raised to reveal the two sinister Red Top match heads.

general service and overhaul, that's a pretty normal request - just one of the 50,000 that have passed though our doors.

However this one was different, this had a sinister mystery to it.

It belonged to an Army Officer who used it for typing up his private Top Secret notes, these were letters he would prefer to type himself so that he could be sure of maximum security.

After we had serviced the machine the man returned to collect it. "How was it, every thing ok?" he asked.

"Yes" I replied, but there is one thing I am not sure about. You had two red top matches fixed into the ribbon lift, (as seen in the picture) why was that?" (Red Top's flare up with only light friction).

He looked thunderstruck, his jaw dropped as he took in what I had said. Looking at the photo he exclaimed: "My God! They almost got through to us." He went on to explain: "I was in a military establishment in Afghanistan where I would often work in a very dangerous explosive environment". Before anyone could enter the building guards would search us for any form of ignition such as matches or cigarette lighters, anything that could cause a spark. I was allowed to take in my non-electric portable typewriter which I would work on in my small office.

"What has that got to do with the red top matches?" I asked. Again he looked stunned. "It must have been a failed act of sabotage, someone knew of my movements and that I was working in a spark-free area. They must have fixed my typewriter so that the friction of the ribbon lift going up and down would ignite the red tops with the intention of blowing up the entire Army Camp."

We both agreed, this was a simple but brilliant attempted act of sabotage, one which was set up secretly by an unseen foe. It was a mystery to the Officer as to who the plotter was and it was a mystery to me as to why the red tops did not ignite.

10) We had a customer recently, who claimed he had been abducted by aliens. But he could not tell us too much as they were listening to him - well who knows?

11) I remember another chap, an elderly and friendly accountant, whose house had the floor in every room full with stacks of clients' papers, accumulated over the years. He worked on a tiny coffee table in the middle of this mess.

The connection with me was that he had borrowed from the shop an expensive electronic typewriter while his was in for repair. Unfortunately, on his way home, while standing at the bus stop, he put the typewriter which was in a large carry case down and decided to go and look in the windows of some adjacent shops.

"Lo and behold," he said, "when I turned round the typewriter had gone."

Obviously it had not jumped on a bus. It was pretty obvious that a passerby saw the unattended case and decided to give it a new home - or had it been abducted by aliens?

It had a value of about three hundred pounds and by misfortune the accountant had been rendered uninsured and penniless by a failed share deal. Needless to say, it became my misfortune.

12) There was the man who aggressively marched into the shop, plonked down two tape cassettes and started to complain that they were both faulty and didn't work correctly. I looked at them and said: "Of course they don't work, they are both fully used up. You need to replace them with some new ones."

With that he curses, marches out, jumps in his car, winds down the window and dumps the worn cassettes on the pavement. Now, I am the sort of bod who considers: that is not the correct thing to do. I just had time to pick them up and drop them through the open sunroof of his car as he was driving off.

13) One unusual sale occurred when an Italian man came into the shop to purchase one of my antique typewriters - an early Italian made Olivetti. After checking it over he said he would like to buy it but only if he could pay for it with leather jackets.

The tale he told was that he travelled back and forth between Italy and England each month importing leather jackets. But, now on his way home, he still had four left. These he would like to exchange for the typewriter. They were well made so a deal was done and he left a happy man.

As for me, I now had four jackets which I needed to find homes for. I put them on display and eventually all were sold. An interesting experiment in a new line of products, but not one I would do again.

14) Many faults on machines are operator faults. One major manufacturing company once reported that seventy-eight per cent of the faults on its machines were user caused. Maybe it was a cover story for their dodgy machines. However, quite a few faults are actually customer based. For example: one of our postal customers recently returned a transcription machine foot-control, stating that his secretary was having a problem with it.

We examined it and no fault could be detected, so we

posted off a new one to him. A week or so later, a parcel arrived from the same people at out door with an apologetic letter: Sorry! It was the secretary! Look at what she has done to this foot control. She *will* sit with an electric fanheater right by her feet. If you look you'll see she has managed to melt this one. Please bill me and send another one.

15) We have customers from the Film industry, Theatre companies and the BBC. The request is usually for a working vintage typewriter. Some time ago the BBC, who are very precise with props, asked me for a certain model of a 1960's manual typewriter it was for use in a documentary they were making about a mass murderer.

The murderer was the serial killer Dr Shipton, who typed up all his notes on this particular model the BBC were asking me for. He was caught by the police when they discovered he had typed out and forged the Will of a patient he had killed. The doctor should have destroyed the typewriter, little did he know that typed letters and numbers are like fingerprints and can be identified and traced to the actually machine used.

It follows that we sometimes aid the police and private detective agencies in their enquiries. We have often been called upon to identify certain transcipts and letters typed on a specific typewriter, ones that will lead them to identify fraud.

16) Typewriters are designed and made by teams of highly-skilled personel. Much is done to ensure the machines perfection in manufacture. However, I think what appears to happen next is they go to people who design all the bits and pieces of packaging. Huge efforts are undertaken to ensure the machines do not come to grief in transit. So these packing bits and pieces are pushed here, there and everywhere around the machine.

Unfortunately, the designers fail to realise that not everyone is as clever and the more paraphernalia which needs removing, the more chance there is of machine damage while unpacking it.

The worst example I have come across was one day when I received a phonecall: "I want a new portable manual which works - can you help?"

"Well, of course I can," I reply. "What's the problem?"

"I have had one after another, in all four portable typewriters from a large high street company. Each one was broken when I unpacked them."

I asked him the make and model and as soon as he told me, I knew he was the problem - not the typewriter! This model was one of the finest ever made, rarely did they go wrong. I told him to come and see me.

Of course, these machines were beautifully made, but full of useless transport packaging, an excess of plugs, bands, clips and other unnecessary bits, it is an art to unpack without causing damage. No wonder so many machines are returned to the suppliers as broken.

We never sell a machine without first unpacking it, removing all the bits and bobs, setting it up and then producing a sample test sheet. That way we have zero returns. The strange thing is, I have sent thousands of my recondition machines all around the world without any of these packing bits and I have never heard of any damage caused by their absence.

17) We have many customers who have health problems, disabilities and ailments with their eyes, ears, lungs, limbs, bowels, bladders and aging brains to name a few.

We have modified typewriters to suit the blind. It is fairly simple, all we do is drill a hole in specific keys and glue in a pinhead. The operator can feel the pinheads and then knows the keyboard layout, and off they go typing away - amazing stuff!

Our most common request daily is: "Do you have a really simple typewriter that I can understand and use?"

18) A customer came in one day and we could see that he had no co-ordination with his limbs. He sat down in order to try out a typewriter his arms and legs moving all out of control. But somehow he managed to steady his hands on the keyboard and type.

"I can see you have a problem, but you're doing all right," I said encouragingly.

"What problem is that?" he replied.

Well, that's life! To me he was a muddle, but to him it was just another day - so what's the problem?

19) I have had many customers who realise their number's up soon and they do not have long with us. The urge to relate their life history is very strong. I have delivered numerous typewriters and also dictation machines to many bed-bound people whose only desire left is to record the tales of their moment in time.

20) Many of our customers are of the legal and law professions. I feel that their type of business often makes them mean and most careful when it comes to expenditure, particularly on new equipment.

The worst I can recall was a lady lawyer who took five months to pay for three large expensive IBM office typewriters. All requests for payment were met with silence. It was only after I asked her office receptionist if the staff were being paid - as we were not - that three days later we received our payment.

Perhaps the answer was not to go in at the top, but go in at the bottom and let the staff anxiety for their jobs and wages rise to the top.

21) Another lawyer customer, likeable, though a bit nutty, called on us to collect a repaired machine. He opened his briefcase, wrote out a cheque for payment, then he went back to his car which was parked nearby. Off he drove.

A few minutes later, I happened to look out of the window and on the pavement, where his car had been, was a very expensive leather briefcase. I quickly retrieved it, fortunately before one of the local lads did, and looked inside - and yes, it was full of court case files.

An hour later a very shattered and distraught lawyer shot through the door. I held up the briefcase and the beam of joy on his face was a pleasure to see.

22) Another we knew was a bit of a tense fellow, but quite agreeable until one day he lost his cool. He slammed the door so hard on his way out that it almost shattered the plate-glass window. The tale here is that he had purchased second-hand machines and new machines. When old and new are in the same office a strange condition can strike the staff. It is what's known as "machine fever."

Strange but true, development of unusual faults in equipment can appear to be man-made more often female-made emotional or jealousy based, purposefully executed to obtain a new machine.

I can well imagine the scene as a maturer staff member with a many year's old one suddenly see the boss's young blue-eyed girl using a fancy new one. It is a fact of life that many staff will complain constantly about their old machine until they get a new one.

Now, back to the slamming door. The reason this chap lost his cool was because he did not know what to do. His secretary was complaining about her typewriter and so he brought it to us. We could never find any serious faults to repair and the machine was going backwards and forwards. He did not realise machine fever had infected his office and the only cure was to invest and update in some more new ones - which he eventually did, it was only then that the balance in the office was restored.

23) We do our utmost to make our reconditioned machines look and operate as new. It is not always achievable - but try we do. It can be very rewarding to have someone say it looks lovely, it looks brand new, but would you believe

there can be times and places where the reverse applies.

A local structural engineering company that we deal with asked me to help with one of its oversea's contacts. It had a large construction order taking place in China and several Chinese engineers were in England working on design details.

One Chinese man before returning to China, wanted to buy a small manual typewriter with the English keyboard layout. As I deal regularly with this company, its chief engineer knew I would have a machine to suit. The Chinese chap arrived and studied my display of reconditioned machines but he said none were good enough because they all looked like new. I was taken aback by this line of thinking and told him I did not understand what he meant.

"I cannot take one back to China that looks like new," he said. "I would be punished - it would be above my station."

I began to understand - this was the time of the communist Red Guard and Chairman Mo's Little Red Book, which laid down what was what. Men like the one I was talking to could not have something better that his boss might have.

"So this typewriter you want to buy would be just the job if it did not look so good?" I asked him.

"Yes," he replied.

"Hang on a minute," I said. "I will soon sort that out."

I took the typewriter to the service bench, picked up a hammer, knocked a few dents in places that caused no harm, then rubbed a file on the corners, gave a few scratches to the body and the typewriter looked rough enough for him to take back to China.

It looked sad on the outside, but inside it was like new. It was a happy Chinaman beaming with delight that I waved goodbye to!

24) My visiting African buyers seem to be in a different world to me. They work on a different clock and calender than I am used to. I would often receive a phone call asking if I had 10 or 20 of this or that make of machine. If I had, we would normally arrange an appointment for a certain time in the day and on a certain day in the week, which seemed fairly straightforward and would be the most convenient to both parties. For instance, we might agreed on say: Tuesday morning at ten o'clock. However, more often than not, they would turn up on a totally different day and time - perhaps at four on a Thursday afternoon. One African buyer I met - who was only a few hours late - asked me:

"How do you like dealing with Africans?"

"I think you are all right when you get here, but none of you seem to be able to tell the time. You do not keep your appointments," I replied.

He roared with laughter. "We work on African time, which means that we think we are on time if we arrive on the right day!"

25) Frisky Females, there are some but not many, unlike window cleaners' tales where they seem to be tripping over them every ten minutes. I am afraid my encounters are about one every decade.

Here is one case: A middle aged lady called into our shop one day and selected a typewriter, not by its quality and not by the make or style, but instead by the colour. Well, that suited me, after all a sale is a sale, but it was rather unusual.

"Could I have it delivered to my home?" she requested.

"Of course, that is no problem. I will bring it round at about two this afternoon, is that all right?" I asked.

So at two o'clock I was knocking on the door.

"Come in," said the lady. "Perhaps you would be so kind as to take it upstairs for me, I would like it in my bedroom."

Fine, no problem - I took the machine upstairs.

"Place it on the dressing table, please."

I put it down and we started chatting for quite a while about this and that.

"I think it's time I was off Mrs. Whatever," I said and made a move down the stairs. I reached the front door but found I could not open it.

"Better let me do that", she said as she leaned over me and flicked up the lock pin - she had locked the door to stop the kids coming in.

"There you are, you can open it now, you are in a dangerous house here you know?" Well I had noticed that Mrs. Whatever was no oil painting and I was pretty certain I was not going to be a notch on her bed post, so it was whoosh - and I was off as though I had been shot from a canon.

26) Another time a lady customer brought her typing machine in to the shop for repair. As it was being booked in she asked if it could be delivered to her home after it was fixed. 'Yes that was no problem' I said. We agreed a time between six and seven oclock in the evening two days later.

Two days later the machine repaired as good as new was safely tucked under my arm as I pressed her door bell, which rang in an upstairs flat in a large house.

Come in she said and follow me. As I closed the front door I noticed an upright Hoover vacuum cleaner standing in the corner of the hallway, however this one had a difference. It was battered and bent as though it had been

114

used as a hammer.

Follow me she said again, and doing as I was told I walked up the stairs into her lounge .

"Place my typewriter there please," she said, "I will try it out." She proceeded to check it over from end to end and finely said, that's fine thank you.

Meanwhile, I had been idly wandering around the flat looking at her selection of large paintings on the walls. Well I am not in any way an artist but I could see these were a bit unusual and said so, as I looked at another one, they were all pictures of mass copulation, orgies and alike.

Yes I love them, she said, "look at this one, it's my favourite". Well I was by now becoming a bit shocked.

I am in the home of an attractive young woman of about 25 years of age, I am almost a stranger to her, and yet she is pointing out to me her sexual preferences. "And this is my second favourite", she said again, looking at another painting of a mass sex scene. "I love all the detail" she said, I agreed, just to be one the safe side.

"Would you like to join me in a drink? I always relax with a bit of music and a couple of drinks at this time of day. Perhaps you would like a beer or a whiskey and something to nibble?" she asked with a rye grin.

My brain is weighing all this up, I am in a stranger's living room, it's early evening, we are looking at erotica and I am being asked to stay for a cosy drink or two. Now my brain starts adding to this scene, she might be ticking off a list of positions taken from the scenes of her erotica, and maybe she has me listed as a potential partner for position 25 or maybe 49 or whatever.

She was strangely nice and attractive, but the whole scene was a bit to unusual for me, so I decided it was time to make tracks and to head for home.

"Thanks for the offer" I said, "but I must get going". With that I started going down the stairs, and she was following me.

As we reached the hallway I once again spotted the bent Hoover, and commented that it looked like it had had a hard time. "Oh that, well that's like that because the boyfriend I have just broken up with is jealous of all I do. The other day he rang my door bell, as I opened the door, he sprang into the hallway grabbed the Hoover went to the car parked outside my flat and beat it up, the windows were stowed in, the doors even the headlamps were smashed, then he threw the Hoover at me and was off not to be seen since".

"What did your new boy friend say about having his car smashed up?" I asked.

"Not much" she replied, "as it was not his car, the smashed up car belonged to someone visiting my next door neighbour".

I was now certain it was time to move on.

"Goodbye" I said, glancing left and right to ensure I was not on the ex-boyfriends hit list.

27) One day a lady phoned the shop to ask if we had available a certain make of typewriter that she was looking to buy.

"Yes we have that in stock," I replied. She agreed our price was competitive and ordered one asking for it to be delivered to her home address.

"Fine I will drop it in about six o'clock tonight, if thats okay?" It was so just after six I knocked on her door, and it opened to reveal the lady of the house. She was about 30 years old, attractive but a bit overweight and was wearing something with a much too low neckline. She indicated that I should come in. "You said you would be able to run over the machine with me, so let's unpack it and put it on the table at the end of the stairs."

Unpacked and plugged in I started to show her the fundamentals of the machine.

It was not long before she said: "I must sit down, I am really tired." With that she climbed up a few stairs, sat down and sighed deeply.

I continued to demonstrate the new machine, but this is where it became difficult to concentrate. She would keep leaning forward to see what I was showing her, however her low neck line did little to hold in her body bits, which were somewhat large.

Every time I showed her another feature, she would lean so far forward I almost felt I should catch them before they fell out. This was making life somewhat difficult, but there was worse to come.

After a short time she appeared restless and as she fidgited around, her legs started moving from a modest knees together 12 o'clock position, to a rather immodest ten minutes to two position. This of course was revealing a site best left unseen.

Life was becoming more difficult, the machine was expensive and quite complicated, I had agreed to showing her the fundamentals of it, but what with her large bits swinging wildly and her legs getting wider, my ability to teach was becoming weakened by the minute.

Time to go, I thought, before she gets too excited and falls off the stairs. I made my farewells and returned to a calmer way of life.

After this encounter, which could have been on her part, shear carelessness or was it a positive act of seduction. I do not know, what I do know was that from then on I would, when possible, take one of my children with me, for them it would be a ride out with dad, for me a bit of insurance.

28) I can recall another time. When I visited a lady at her house late one evening to buy some redundant typewriters that she had offered me. I entered the room where they had been stored and checked them over.

"Yes, they are just the job," I told her.

We agreed a price, I payed her straight away and loaded them into my estate car. There were ten office manual typing machines and I had no doubt they would end up somewhere in Africa. We then stood by the car chatting for over two hours mainly about her life roaming the world from a young age. She was a lovely-looking woman with all the womanly bits of the right size and in the right places.

Her husband was away working abroad for six months.

"How about coming back in for a coffee?" she offered suddenly, with a slight change in the tone of her voice, one that my already heightened senses picked up on.

Well, it was half past ten in the evening and although our two hours chat had been charming and a real pleasure, I had a feeling she was getting more frisky than thirsty. I had a fine wife and two lovely young kids at home, so with a very regretful" no thanks," I was in the car and off - but she was a beautiful woman. The thought comes to me at times, maybe I missed the finest "cup of coffee" that will ever come my way?

29) We received an order to supply a new typewriter to a monastery in Sussex and was asked would we deliver it. One of our young sales staff made an appointment and arrived at the agreed time. A knock on the door produced a monk and our sales chap explained that he wished to meet with Abbot Kelvin.

"Follow me," said the monk. They went into an office where the monk indicated to an eletric socket then handed him a piece of paper and said: "Show me how it works."

Over an hour later he said: "Right, unplug it and follow me. I will now take you to Abbott Kelvin, the monk you have really called to see."

I suppose if you are spending your life in such a limited restricted way, spending an hour with a stranger and a piece of new technology, was too big a thrill for the old monk to miss.

30) Apart from typewriters and dictation machines we also purchase used high quality office chairs from the bank my friend works for. These I can re-upholster and sell on, usually at half the price of a new one - but they look as good as new once their refurbishment is complete.

One day I received a telephone call from "Bob the Buyer":

"I'm disposing of twenty office chairs, make an offer and I'd be pleased to let you have them."

"Right, I will be be there in one hour, Bob."

I arrived and was shown the goods. I made an offer which was gladly accepted, especially as they urgently needed the space. I loaded ten of the chairs into my estate car and drove out of their carpark heading back to my shop.

Unfortunately, as I drove out, I failed to remember the existence of their two foot high, twenty foot long, boundary wall. I heard a crunch thought: hello, what's that? Getting out of the car I realised I had hit their wall and damaged my car door, well that's what comes of rushing. I was in a hurry having promised to clear the remaining ten chairs that afternoon and time was getting tight.

Cursing I drove off.

Not far, properly 30 yards or so when I checked my rearview mirror. oh, no, I could not believe it how I did not see it I don't know, but there it was, the bank's proud wall twenty foot long, demolished, lying flat on the pavement. It looked like I was doing a hit and run on a wall, but the truth was I had not noticed it. Well, it's down now, I thought, best if I carry on and unload the chairs at the shop and go back and own up.

An hour later, on my return to the bank for the remaining chairs, two security guards immediately pounced: "Got you, you're the one that knocked our wall down and drove off, we have you now."

Luckily, Bob the Buyer came to my rescue he believed my story and admitted the wall must have been weak anyway. Good old Bob.

31) Bowels and bladders - we all have them and some are tricky to get on with sometimes. Here are a few shop encounters of this nature, skip them if you're about to eat your supper but these are true stories from the Typewriter Shop.

It is a strange thing to notice, but it is a fact that almost all of my friendly buyers from Africa ask to use the toilet. Now I don't know if this is ancient custom or what, but ask they do. My mechanic reckons it's a tribal thing, something like marking your territory to keep competitors away, but I think it could be due to our colder climate.

32) It was Derby Day at the nearby Epsom Horse Race Course, Elizabeth and I were quietly gazing out of the shop window at the busy passing road traffic heading there, when we noticed a privately hired double decker Bus had stopped outside the car repair garage across the road opposite our showroom.

Two men emerged from the bus and went into the garage

were they asked if they could use the toilet. The garage owner said that was okay, but what he did not know, (but was soon to find out), there were 80 or 90 more men to follow.

The first two returned to the bus, and the top deck started to trundle down and began to form a long line with the lower deck joining in. It took over one hour before the bus was on its way.

33) Mr Smelly - he earned his nickname well enough. He was an elderly man who called on us for a typewriter repair. He was in the strangest condition we have ever seen and we've had plenty of odd ones.

He was fat, fifty plus, and was wearing full women's make-up, women's jewellery - necklace, earrings and so on. He was also wearing a bright pink jacket. His body - the top half - he had taken great care over, strange that it was. His top half dressed like a prima donna, his bottom half I shall decline from detailing. Suffice it to say, it was in a dreadful state. It looked like he had fouled his britches many times by the look of them. Yet he was not the least bit bothered.

He smelled so bad, my secretary, trapped at her desk in the corner unable to escape, sat there going cross-eyed. I quickly took the situation in hand. I decided I would suggest he goes to another repair shop, one I had reasons to dislike. So I picked up his machine and gasped: "I will put this in your car and direct you to another repairer."

As I loaded it, I spotted a sad little dog on the front seat who seemed to be saying help me. As I gave directions, the dog was still looking at me despairingly, so all I could do was to stroke his head and say good luck boy. As the man drove away he turned out of our service road onto the duel carriageway. However he turned his car onto the nearside fast-lane and straightforward head-on into a stream of cars coming towards him. Screeching brakes, much cursing and shouting, but fortunately, no collision. A swift turn back into the service road and after some redirection, he and his dog went successfully on their way.

34) We have, over the years dealt with many Keyboard Training Schools and Colleges, acting as their machine supplier and also their maintenance team. Some schools had contracts with us whereupon we would call twice yearly to service some 60 to 70 machines in their classrooms and the school offices.

On one such visit, teacher Miss Murphy,, was showing me the machines in her classroom that needing attention."This is the last one, over here on the floor she said."

We both crouched down to examine the machine when

suddenly the classroom appeared to fill with the sounds of Wagner, which gradually faded to a gentle Mozart rendition. No - it wasn't the music room in use - I'm afraid Miss Murphy's large lunch was on pay-back time. Being a gentleman and fearing an encore, I turned a deaf ear to the blast, and totally ignoring the situation, I picked up the machine. "I'll take this one to our workshop, I'm off now Goodbye, Miss Murphy."

35) A customer needed a reliable reconditioned manual to type up his studies for the following year. A standard request - but with a difference - his was a study in anthroplogy. Plans had been arranged and a grant obtained; he was to live on a remote primitive island off the coast of New Guinea in the Pacific Ocean.
Somewhat apprehensive of the experience, he explained his adventure, and added that the only contact with the outside world would be twice yearly via a government boat. There would be no electricity, medical care, telephones, and so forth, he would live and eat as a native. The island's Chief had given permission for the study of his tribe and their way of life.
"What if he offers me his favourite wife, and I cant satisfy her. You know they were headhunters only a few years ago. I don't fancy ending up as their Sunday lunch" he said in a half joking shaky voice.
What a plucky young man, I hope he came back.

36) A couple came in the shop looking for a typwriter for the wife's ailing father. A simple machine was required, which narrowed the search to two different makes - one was more expensive than the other. The wife wanted the dearer one, whereas the husband clearly thought otherwise. All of a sudden he produced from his pocket a piece of string with a leaded bob weight attached to one end. Holding this device he swung it over each machine and announced to the wife that the cheaper machine was giving the best vibes. And that was the best one for old dad. She quite happily accepted his so called magical powers. So dad ended up with the cheaper, older machine. This seems to me to be a pretty useful tool for most men to have in their pockets when on shopping sprees with the wife I must get one!.

37) Over the years we have met many authors and budding authors. Some are mums who nurse a desire to write children's books, others have been military men and women who feel the need to write down their encounters. Many others, like the novelist, have a tale to tell and a burning desire to make a million pounds or two. Then

there are the playwrights, the journalists and the professional writers, among these are still many who feel the familiar tap, tap, tap sound of the keys on a manual typewriter; more safisfying and less confusing than working on a modern and complicated electronic keyboard or computer.

I always enjoy meeting people and listening to their enthusiasm to write. To these tryers I always give an encouraging push and mention several books I find useful they are called the Writers' and Artists' book, the Writers' handbook, and Writers' Market book, these are all yearly publications.

To these potential writers, if you are one of them - I wish you good luck

38) I am afraid some of our recollections are of a critical nature. I guess they are the ones that rivet themselves into the mind. The vast majority of our customers are pleasant and charming. Here is one fellow who is just that.

He is an eighty-four year old, retired priest who has been calling on us, typewriter in hand, for a good many years now. Despite his age, he whips around always with a joke to tell, his latest is.

A man goes into the local Newspaper Office to place an advertisement in the paper's personal column. He askes the assistant what the cost would be and she replies:

"Five pounds a word, Sir."

"Oh dear," he says, "I can only spare fifteen pounds - so I will just have three words."

He fills in the form and writes - Doris is Dead.

The girl looks shocked and says:

"That's rather blunt - I will ask the Manager if he can help you, perhaps he can do you a special deal."

The girl comes back. "The Manager said you may have up to six words for the same price."

"Oh, great," said the customer. "Will you please place this advertisement then: DORIS IS DEAD - TYPEWRITER FOR SALE.

39) Some time back, twenty five years or so, when modern manual typewriters were very expensive and we still sold the black Royals and Imperials, we had a customer place an order for eight of this type.

"Must be the old, black reconditioned typewriters," he said.

"Oh, and cheap."

We settled on a price that satisfied us both and arranged delivery for the following Sunday morning.

The chap lived in Hampstead Heath in London and Sunday morning came and I delivered the machines. I asked him why he needed eight.

"Simple," he replied, "it's because I have eight children. They will have a machine each and a private tutor and they will all learn to type together."
That's efficiency for you!

40) Now for the opposite in efficiency. A young lady brought her typewriter in for repair asking if we could do this, that and the other to get it working properly. I told her we certainly could and it would be ready in two or three days. The job was done and the machine sat on our rack waiting for its owner to collect it and take it home.

As I have already stated, we have little space to store machines and we're always under pressure to achieve a twenty-four hour turnaround. In this case the weeks went by, then months were ticked off. After three months and two letters, a personal visit to her home revealed that she had moved away with no forwarding address.

The rule on abandoned machines is if unclaimed and the owner untraceable, after six months they can be scrapped or sold to recover incurred costs. This we finally had to do.

Well, almost two years later, this young lady called in to collect her machine. She was somewhat surprised to learn that she cannot abandon possessions for years and expect them to still be there when she returned.

41) One day a man from Birmingham, which is a four hundred mile round trip from our shop, phoned me five or six times asking about a particular typeface and typewriter that he wanted. After repeatedly getting nowhere, I was fed up with his constant calls and suggested strongly he should go elsewhere as I was unable to help him. He seemed to take this badly.

The next day the shop phone rang. "We are on our way to see you" he said, in not too polite a tone.

Life in the shop it seemed was about to get a bit tough.

A few hours later in strolled two determined rough-looking men with their good-looking women and two spotty toddlers. The kids immeditately demanded drinks, and in a flash were handing two cans of pop. These youngsters tore back the ring-pulls, parked their rears on the shop doorstep and promptly guzzled away. Meanwhile, the two men were scrutinising every machine on display.

After an hour or two, "this will do the job " they said finally as they picked one out.

They paid up and as they were loading the typewriter into their car, I casually asked. "You seem very particular as to your typeface - why is that?"

"Well" they explained, "there are certain cheque recogniton machines which can only read one specific typeface and thats the one we want."

With that they drove away.

What was their game who can tell? Villains at work - I would guess.

42) Over the years I have placed many items for sale in local auction rooms and also London based ones, these are only half an hour's train ride away from the shop. This tale is about one of my London visits.

Some years ago a good friend had given me a couple of small framed oil paintings, they were about the size of an A4 sheet of paper, which happens to be a convenient size to fit into my very old briefcase which I used to transfer them from our shop office, where they had hung for a number of years, up to the London auction rooms.

Following a change to the office decor, the two had been consigned out of sight into a remote cupboard.

One day, the thought came to me to try and find out who the artist was and maybe I could pass them on to someone else who would like to display them. My research through various reference books showed me that they were painted by a known artist. Armed with this name and a limited amount of knowledge, I telephoned Sotherby's Auction Rooms in London and asked the receptionist to put me through to the relevant expert. After some discussion I eventually asked for a valuation. Over the telephone the expert was able to confirm the artist as a well known name and indicated a value which was obtained from recent sales of the artist's work. Whilst the pictures were not rare they were, to some people, very collectable and had a combined estimated value of £2500. Now that to me said, sell them instead of letting them lie about out of sight filling up a cupboard.

A few weeks later Elizabeth and I took the train to London with the intention of taking these two pictures to Sotherby's Auction Rooms. Upon arrival we unloaded our cargo onto their "Booking In" table where all of our details were written down, a reference number handed to us, together with the date of the next relevant auction sale.

It was still early in the day so we agreed to spend the rest of the day in town taking in the shops and the sites of our marvellous city. Walking around all day with my extra large worn out briefcase I now no longer wanted was becoming a nuisance. Unfortunately I could not find anywhere to dispose of it and I definitely could not abandon it as this was the time when the IRA were very active. Any case left on its own would cause a major incident so reluctantly my worthless case hang heavy on my arm all day. Eventually we decided it was time to return to the shop. On the long walk back to the main railway station, we passed a Chinese Restaurant which had for sale, hanging on racks in the window, a dozen or so cooked, and glazed Peking ducks. "They look tasty," I said to Elizabeth.

"Let's have one for dinner tonight," she agreed. So one was bought and carefully placed in my now needed briefcase. This duck and a fine wine tonight should restore us I thought to myself.

Half an hour later the train arrived at our home station. Here we began the five minute walk to our parked car. On the way I stopped to look in the window of a camera shop. Suddenly I felt hot breath on the back of my neck and a rough male voice saying," I think you should give me your brief case." Now the thought of giving up my no longer wanted brief case was okay but giving up my newly acquired dead duck was not to my liking. I was faced with a tricky situation, to my front my head was only six inches away from a thick plate glass window, to my left there was a heavy sales advertisement board and behind me a bad breathed, rough sounding male suggesting I give him my case, which he probably thought was full of valuables, like banknotes, diamonds and gold. He would never have guessed in a million years his reward in this hold-up would only be a dead duck.

"Give me your Case," I heard his rough voice repeat, I also heard Elizabeth pleading, saying to me "Come away -come away" which I would have been only too pleased to do but the stranger had me penned in. I calculated: there was no way forward, no way to the left or backwards. Then I remembered, always in a tight spot try to avoid eye contact so turning around was not the answer.

Being an Englishman who was born and bred in a tough area, giving in to intimidation is a difficult thing for me to do, so, standing my ground and continuing to look through the window at the cameras on display, I replied: "No I do not think I will." This, of course was a most incredibly stupid thing to say. Giving up the unwanted briefcase meant I would only be losing a dead duck. I was standing up against a foe I could not even see, which could result in me ending up as dead as the duck. I could have received a knife in the back, or my head slammed against the plate glass window, I could not offer any defence and definitely no retaliatory action from the trapped position I was in. I, therefore, could only act defiant and all I could do was to bluff it out, I stood there expecting the worst, tightly clutching my case and my dead duck, when the rough voice a few inches away breathed on me again and said "Think yourself a lucky man." And with that he and a second man backed down; and were off on their way.

Later that evening at dinner the duck, he served us well, and later that month, the paintings, they sold well, and as for me, well I know, I was a lucky man.

43) Another tale about eye contact and violence. While unloading machines from my estate car and taking them into the shop, I was aware of a fast driven car that pulled around me very close as the driver drove it through the narrow side road between my shop and the next door nursery school. It was clear he had mistaken the driveway for a short cut, which it was not, it was in fact a dead end.

A moment later I am still unloading as the mad driver roared up the alleyway in reverse and at full speed. At the same time a young schoolgirl was walking past the shops, I could see she would reach the gap as the speeding car in reverse came through and she was in serious danger. I leaped forward waving my arms to slow down the mad driver. The girl had seen my gesture and just in time had managed to divert herself away from the scene. The driver had reached the end of the alleyway and his tether, he leaped out of the car screaming abuse and headed for me in an extremely threatening manner. Now I was positioned some 30 feet away from the shop window, in between unloading trips, when he came at me. My position was again tricky, he was half my age, big and tough. Trying to fight off a highly strung individual was beyond my ability and strength. However, I could not allow myself to be seen by Elizabeth looking out through the window and my neighbours looking out of their shops, to be so weak as to turn and run, which would have been the sensible thing to do. What I actually did, I am glad to say seemed to work. I did not run neither did I show any aggression and I definitely did not make any eye contact. I strode right up towards him expecting to get beaten up but my instinct and pride gave me a strong fast pace. As I met him, his rage was consuming him. He presumed I was chastising him for fast driving in and out of our driveway. He drove in like a madman and drove out even worse. It seems my non aggression and non eye contact unhinged and bewildered him. Moving in and standing as close to him as I could he suddenly turned his abuse from me onto my new car as he said, move the ** fancy car out of my way you **- ** and with that he was back in his car and was off. The young schoolgirl had safely long gone and I was still in one bit. I could not believe my luck - I still think it was down to not making eye contact.

I do believe if you cant control the outcome of events you can still control your dignity and behaviour.

44) For some years one of the flats above a shop in our parade, was rented out to a variety of tenants. One lady held the tenancy for a number of months, during that time

she would often call into the shop for a friendly chat with me. This was at the time of the jimmy riddlers. I had started to replace the old wooden end part of our building with a solid brick extension, which was to be, at that time, on the ground floor only.

One very hot summer weekend, I was working on the site when I noticed the young lady leaving her flat and going down the road to the local food shops.

An hour or so later, I was working inside the new dusty extension which had just reached ceiling height, when I heard a soft voice saying "hello," then again another "Hello," I looked all around, still not seeing anyone, and then I spotted the source, my word, what a beauty, I immediately thought.

The soft hello was coming from the outside of the extension through a gap in the brickwork which had been left open in order to eventually form a small three ft wide by two ft high window. In the centre of this gap was the face of the lady from the flat. I noticed instantly there was a difference to how she had looked an hour before. She had come back from the shops and had undergone a major smarting up act. Now she was elegantly dressed, hair and makeup looking perfect, and, framed by the gap in the brickwork, she looked stunning.

Suddenly she spoke, "I was wondering," she said slowly," it is very hot and dusty for you in their, is there anything at all I could do for you, or would you like to take a break and come into my place for a cool drink?"

That's a very nice and friendly thing to say, I thought.

My problem was, if she had said that an hour ago, it would have seemed all right. But now I had noticed she had changed her appearance from a bit unkempt to really looking splendid. She had changed all her clothes, hair and make-up perfect I thought she was looking as good as it gets.

It might just be for refreshments, I thought, but my male instincts were saying there could be more being offered here than tea and cake. Her offer either way was very tempting. However there was "more" to the scene.

From were she stood all she could see was myself looking back at her. As we exchanged glances I could feel my chemistry being stirred up.

Unbeknown to her there was a third party present, directly between the two of us, siting on a wooden box, low down under this part built window space was my 14 year old son who was helping me with the building work.

She was not aware there were three of us and was looking at me with a belladonna look in her eyes, she was also looking at me for an answer, whereas twelve inches below her face was another face, that of my son who was looking at me in a disapproving way. As for me I am looking at her with a terrible yearning to take up her refreshment offer

My reply was, thank you very much I really appreciate it, but I must finish this job of work today. She just nodded and with out a word turned away, I decided she was after all, being friendly and not frisky. However it was strange?. After that visit on that very hot summer's day she never came into the shop for a chat with me ever again.

45) An order for one hundred used manual typewriters came in. The customer was an African man with a business in England. His homeland was Zimbabwe but he had obtained a contract to supply one hundred used machines to Somalia.

The typewriters were to be manual machines of any make or size, office machines or portable, it did not matter as long as they were cheap.

We turned out all the cupboards, looked under the benches, it was time for a clear out, so that's what it became. In the end we could only find sixty-eight to suit. I contacted all my friends who have similar businesses. One of them set to and dug and delved in every corner. He managed to find seventeen machines which I bought off him. This made eighty-five typewriters now available.

During my discussions with the oversea's buyer, he had told me that he already had three machines in his possession which, added to my eighty-five, made eighty-eight. Not bad but still twelve short and nowhere else to obtain the rest. I don't like an uncompleted job; but we were stuck. However, we still had two or three days to go before shipping date.

I have found many times that if you try hard, then fate often gives a hand. The next day would you believe, the phone rang - my secretary took the call:

"There is a man on the telephone asking if you know anybody who would like some old manual typewriters they are disposing of?"

I was on the phone in a flash. The caller was a complete stranger to me. He was from the Natural History Museum in London.

"I have twelve old manual typewriters we are replacing and wondered if they were worth anything," he said. "If you do not want them they can go in the rubbish skip."

"Hold on! Don't do that, I can find them a new home. I'm afraid they are not worth much, but I will send you a cheque for one hunded pounds and a driver will collect this afternoon. I am really pleased to have your offer."

The driver whipped the twenty miles to London, loaded up the machines and brought them back to join the others in my store room. Now my ninety-seven machines and Addas's the buyer's three others, made up the hundred which were required. Whoopee! Just made it!

Apparently these machines were going to Somalia, they would be sent to one hundred individual remote villages where a selected person would be trained as a typist and they and their machine would, in future, communicate with officialdom by means of the printed word. The world of writing was coming their way.

46) This tale I remember was about an export order. Six manual typewriters were needed at a mission station in the African Congo. They were to be supplied to six nuns working there.

My trouble was, at that moment in time, our stock of typewriters of the right type was very low. In fact, we only had six machines that would fit the bill. However, that sounds okay, but the trouble was five of the machines were running perfectly, but the sixth one kept developing strange faulty habits. Although it was working, we could not get it to our usual high standard.

Shipping day came and like it or not, we had to include this odd machine with its five other cousins. I just hope the nun using it could arrange for some Divine Help!

47) When people are testing a machine to see if it suits their touch, they often type subconscious thoughts of what's passing through their minds as they sit there. Odd one line strange remarks are often typed. Here are a few examples.

1) Hello John, how are your feet today?

2) This typewriter really feels good, I like it.

3) I do hope Judy can lose weight.

4) I did not know a typewriter shop could be so exciting. (On this occasion we were having some strong words with another customer who was aggressive and seemed to be trying to pull a fast one.)

5) It is Uncle Fred's birthday. I must bake him a cake.

6) The quick brown fox jumps over the lazy dog. (This covers all the keyboard letters.)

7) Now is the time for all good men to come to the aid of the party. (This is a standard quote.)

8) I like this typewriter, I shall be able to write some good stories on this.

9) What shall I get hubby and kids for dinner tonight?

10) I am so pleased to find a machine I can understand. (This is the most common line typed.)

48) Some of our tales occur on the outside of the shop premises This one is about the refuge collection service by the local council for the flats and the shopping parade. For

two years I have been complaining to the local council about the poor condition of their collection vehicle.

When these vehicles collect the waste from the large wheeled bins used by the car repairers in their workshops which are situated behind the back of the shops, what happens is, as the rubbish it tipped into the vehicle, foul toxic liquid pours out through bad or worn seals on to the road washing through many sharp objects such as nuts, bolts, screws, small motor parts and a variety of metal objects. The collection vehicle moves off leaving behind a large puddle of the foul liquid which is then sprayed onto people and parked cars as other fast moving cars drive through it. The metal parts cause tyre wear and punctures.

After two years and many letters of complaint, along with photographs illustrating the problem, the council have finally replaced the vehicle on our route with a new one --but where has the old one gone to?

49) If you are not in the world of using computers, then worry not, as you are not alone. The most common request we have daily is: "Have you in stock a simple typewriter?" Often it is a man or woman trying to find a writing machine that the arthritic fingers and ageing memory skills of their old mum or dad can understand and use. There are many other people of all ages who feel embarrassed and often excuse themselves to us with statements such as: "The house is full of computers, but I still use my old manual portable typewriter." Many people feel inadequate in not being part of our computer laden society, but the truth is; if they only want to type straightforward letters, then you cannot beat a straightforward typewriter.

50) Most of the people we meet are decent, there are only a few who are nasty but there are quite a few who are fools and sometimes cocky fools. Any differences we have with our customers are generally resolved in a sensible, mutually agreeable and pleasant way. However, one clash proved different.

One day a newly established legal company came to us for several reconditioned dictation machines for their new office. After some six months or so, one of their legal staff brought the machines back and said they did not want them any more and they would like all of their money back and buy, instead, one of our latest typewriters, an IBM machine. I was not pleased as this seemed a bit cheeky and improper. However, I agreed and one of my excellent IBM typewriters went off for use in their office. Three months later the junior solicitor returned the IBM saying it was not working properly and, as such, they would like all of their money back. This in total was some nine months from the start of our original transaction. I informed him that I could not do that and if there was a problem and the machine was still under guarantee, I would get it checked over and adjusted. He replied that this was no good as they did not want the machine any more, and wanted a full refund. After I protested and reminded him that reconditioned machines only have a three month guarantee, yet we were some nine months from the original purchase, he told me to do as he said or he would take me to court and, because it was their game, it would not cost them anything but it would cost me a fortune in time and money.

Now it appeared to me that we had a cocky little smart alec, a young lawyer trying to intimidate me with his legal know how. This was like waving a red flag at a bull. To me he was the equivalent of a young thug in a smart suit. I told him to do what he wished and with that I opened the shop door and sent him on his way. He looked a bit shocked that I had not given in to his legal threats, and he turned round and shouted that I would be sorry and then strode out leaving behind his IBM typewriter.

A few weeks later I received a writ to attend the local small claims court of justice. Attending a legal court room held no fear for me as I had been through the system only two months before and had learnt the ropes. The reason I was acquainted with the court procedure was, I had used the courts for myself having brought a case against someone and, in doing so, I had gained knowledge of how the system worked.

My previous court case was simple, we had taken the family on a week's holiday to Devon. Meanwhile my children's pet cat, Jason was put into the care of the local cattery. Upon our return from holiday we all went to collect our fluffy friend, to bring him home

However, when we arrived we were told by the owner that he was sorry, but the cat seems to have run away. This naturally caused some concern to all of us especially the children. The owner apologised and said he did not know what had happened but the door was open and the cage was empty. He said the only thing he could do to compensate us for our loss was to offer us one of his wife's kittens. Apparently she breeds them and with the next litter he said we could have one. It was sad to lose Jason but I am aware things can go wrong sometimes so "it was no good crying over spilt milk." I said that we should leave it six weeks in case Jason found his way back home to us as animals sometimes do, and if after that time there was no sign of him, I would take up the offer of a kitten. We did the gentleman's handshake to seal the agreement and went home sadly without our old friend. Six weeks later, there was still no sign of our old friend so I telephoned the cattery to tell the man that Jason had not made it back to us and now the children would like one of their kittens to join our family as we had agreed.

My call was answered by the man's wife and when I explained the situation she yelled at me and said I was not having one of her kittens which were very special and my cat was just an old tom of no value. I explained to her that I had been very patient and understanding and it was her obligation to honour the deal suggested by her husband. She shouted again and said I could not have one of her kittens as I had signed a Disclaimer of Responsibility Notice when I had booked our cat into their cattery and there was nothing I could do about it, it was just my bad luck.

Well, I could not believe someone, so clearly in the wrong, could be so rude, ignorant and stupid. They had lost my children's pet cat which I had paid them to look after and now I was being shouted at. I had indeed signed the company's disclaimer when I booked Jason into the cattery, but disclaimers of this nature are for not holding the owner's responsible for cat flu or the like. These disclaimers can cover many things, but one thing they do not cover is negligence, and losing our cat, that they had been paid to look after, was a clear act of negligence. I

had two choices, one to walk away and forget poor old Jason, or the other, to make a claim for our loss through the local small claims court. This is what I decided I should do.

I took the case of the "missing cat" to the local court to get a judgement from the arbitrator who decides who is right and who is wrong in these matters. However, the arbitrator decided that the case of the missing cat was about a special point of law and therefore, we needed to go into the official courtroom. A second court visit was made on another day and after a couple of hours of cross examining, the Judge in his gown and wig, asked the cattery owner what she thought Jason was worth. She stated in her opinion he was worth nothing as he was just an old tom cat with no value. When the Judge asked me, as I stood in the witness box, what I thought the value of the cat was, I could only reply: he was beyond value because he was one of the family. The Judge agreed saying that pets are part of family life and are therefore, valuable. He awarded us damages for their negligence. After all, I had paid them to look after our family pet and they in their incompetence, had lost him and what his fate was to be, sadly, we will never know. The total sum awarded to us was many times more than the value of one of the cattery's precious kittens and I hoped the woman owner had learnt her lesson from it.

This case of poor old, missing Jason was my introduction to local court room drama and it served me well as I was now able to stand up to this young aggressive lawyer and his elder partner who were trying to intimidate me. The day came in court for me to defend myself against these bullying legal men. The outcome was that the chief arbitrator, after hearing both sides of the case, announced that all that was needed to establish the IBM machine's suitability was for each side to obtain an expert witness report. This, of course, was no problem for us, we could soon prove the IBM was working perfectly. The lawyers, realising they had no case, withdrew their claim from the courts, collected the IBM from the shop and were never seen again.

I had won my second court case. However, they come with a cost in as much as it takes a lot of time and effort, also stress and strain but sometimes you have to stand up and fight for what you think is right.

Business, pleasure, travelling, strange people, that is what we have seen and read about so far. Well, the next chapter is completely different, it is a chapter for you, that is if you want it, it is about becoming a collector of our ancient writing machines. If you can type you will love these old machines that maybe your mother, grandmother or even your great grandmother might have used. These old machines in their day would have been adored or hated by the users, whereas today we can love them all for the different styles and designs that come from the effort and skill of those early inventors and engineers, who after centuries of trying finally brought the art of "Clear Writing" into being.

Chapter 14

COLLECTING ANTIQUE TYPEWRITERS

Finding - Buying - Collecting and Selling Antique Typewriters
From £5 to £50,000

Most people that type will love these old machines, It was they that brought the art of "Clear Writing" into being.

Before these machines were invented all writing was done by hand, usually with a birds feather or a dip pen and the results varied wildly as to its illegibility. Unclear writing meant unclear orders of all kinds would occur all to often.

The constant cry for a desk top size type of Printing machine that could produce "clear writing" had been heard since the invention of the Printing Press two century's before. These old writing machines were the answer to that cry.

Okay, so lets say you want to be an "Antique Typewriter Collector". Collectors come in all shapes, sizes and ages.

Let us start with mum, as well as her there could still be grandma and maybe great grandma. There could be daughters, and to their side there could be dad, grandad, maybe great grandad, and possibly sons too. This could, therefore, be a complete family of collectors: eight different age and gender groups, and each group will have different financial and mobility abilities.

Collecting means spending and travelling. It need not be much and it might not be far on the other hand, you could spend huge sums and travel the world to satisfy the urges of a determined collector. You will need to read and learn what is collectable and how much things are worth. There are a number of general antique collectors books in print, or if you are in the computer world, then much information can be found on the internet.

The following pages show a few different types of antique typewriters. My second book in a planned trilogy will show hundreds of the types of writing machines both Antique and Classic; all out there for the collector to find.

So where to hunt? For this treasure let's start with.

CAR-BOOT SALES. These are everywhere most Saturdays and Sundays, but its best to get there early. Some serious collectors and dealers will arrive at the break of dawn when most sellers are still setting up their stands. They are out to spot that one buy that they can maybe retire on, or at least a buy or two that will pay for the next holiday.

If you become experienced, like these early dealers are, you will soon spot a machine that the seller is only too pleased to get rid of. To them making five pounds or so is good stuff, but if you know your machines, it could be worth fifty or even five hundred. So off to the boot sales you go, but make it early, otherwise you will not beat the other guys.

AUCTION ROOMS. If you do not know where your nearest auction rooms is, look in the *Yellow Pages* or a similar phone book. For a yearly subscription of a few pounds, the rooms will send you its Sales' Booklets. These could be weekly, monthly or whatever. My local auction rooms have a sale every Monday morning. I first started going there thirty-odd years ago. I still recall bidding for a *William's* typewriter, quite a rare machine. There was only one other person out for this machine, apart from myself. The bidding jogged up in one pound units up to twenty pounds. Now this might not seem much now, but at that time it was a week's wages for me. I decided I could not go any higher so I dropped out. I discovered some years later, that the same model *William's* typewriter sold in another auction for £4,200 So there you are. You can't win them all!

If you decide you would like to bid for a typewriter in an upcoming auction, then you can leave your maximum bid with the room porter, along with your name and address and, of course, the correct lot number. Make sure he or she writes the correct number down, or you might become the owner of a box containing second-hand bowler hats, or a stuffed frog or something equally as stimulating.

If you decide to attend the auction you don't need to get dressed up in your Sunday best. The rooms are a working environment, many are unheated and can be dirty or, to say the least, scruffy. Some are seated sales, but many can be crowded with standing-room only. By attending the sale you might bid and buy cheaper, but watch you don't get carried away and overspend. Another point when bidding a gentle wave to the auctioneer is enough. Once he has spotted you, he will return until you drop out of the bidding or you end up the buyer. Remember when the bidding is in process don't wave your arms about or scratch your head, otherwise you might end up with that box of bowler hats.

If you are not familiar with auctions I suggest you read the contents of one of their catalogues. You will be surprised at what can be bought and sold.

NEWSPAPER ADVERTISEMENTS. Reading the For Sale columns can sometimes be rewarding. Items of virtually everything are sold in the free and local papers, sometimes even antique typewriters. You could place your own advert in the wanted columns, some advertising is free, but many newspapers will charge to place it.

Responding to private adverts is usually fine, but watch your words. Offering a lower price for the goods is alright, but don't criticise them too much: you must remember the owner might have loved whatever it is for many years. Looking out for and keeping clear of spotty kids is always a good idea. Dodge dogs and cats: dogs can be a nuisance especially the ones that decide to give you a good sniff over, and keep your hand over your vitals if the dog is a big one with - a you shouldn't be here - look. Cats are usually no problem, but don't say can I stroke your pussy, try and just keep to the point, if you like the goods you called to see, make an offer, then get going.

A friend of mine advertised his car for sale in the local newspaper. A chap called to see it and was taken out on a test-drive, then back to the house to discuss the price, history and other things. George, my friend, said It suddenly hit him - the buying man had now been in their company all that Sunday afternoon, including having tea; he had been there for four hours. George realised this wasn't a car purchase - this was somebody who was just filling in his Sunday afternoon and having a free meal as well.

SECOND-HAND SHOPS. These shops sell all sorts of things including old typewriters. Most of the dealers running these shops will know the value of the item they are selling - but not always. I was approached by a dealer in one of these shops a while ago, they were selling an old *Columbia* typewriter for one of their customers. I was offered it for two hundred pounds: "No thanks," I said, "I think I will let this one go. Thanks for offering." When I was looking for a value for another machine a few days later, I noticed a *Columbia* typewriter the same model as the one the dealer offered me, it had sold in auction for two thousand pounds. Dealers, and even myself can miss things. So if you learn your stuff, you may well see a bargain or two.

REFUSE RECYCLING FACILITY. I have found that when I visit the recycling facility I often see something abandoned as waste by another visitor, which to my eye, is valuable. This is a place where one person's rubbish, can be another person's great find.

I can recall a long time ago when the *IBM Golfball* typewriter was every typist's dream machine. I visited my local facility and was depositing a quantity of boxes and old scrap machines, while I was unloading my items I spotted in front of me one of these typewriters which the previous owner had decided was beyond repair. I immediately called the Yardman over and said,

"Could I take this scrapped machine?"

"Sure," he said, but the look in his eye said,

"How about a fiver?"

So that was it, I gave him a fiver, loaded up the *IBM* and off I went. After a full rebuild, it sold for two hundred pounds. It wasn't so much the money that appealed to me - it was the thought of what other great fortunes are to be found in these areas of disposal. From then on I always cast a glance around when I am disposing of my scrap machines, which is usually twice a week. This glancing around has had its rewards. I remember one incident when I was heaving my scrap typewriters on to the waste heap. The yardman standing next to me was tearing open a plastic bag which contained someone's possessions which were, obviously, no longer needed. He fished into the bag and suddenly pulled out a small wooden box encrusted with some 50 intricately shaped metallic mouldings of scenes of wild animals, people and gods.

"That looks interesting," I said.

"It's yours for a couple of pounds," he replied.

I quickly gave over the two pounds and was off. Sometime later I had it valued by one of the large London auction houses.

"Ah, yes," they said as they studied it. "It is a pity it is not the gold version, they are worth a lot of money. Your's is a base metal version, only worth four to five hundred. It is a Japanese made wooden box covered with samurai sword decorations on its top and the four sides. They use all of these intricate shapes to decorate their sword handles."

It is a lovely thing to look at. I use a magnifying glass to see all of the fine detail and I am glad to give it a home.

On another trip I almost tripped over a Victorian wooden writing slope. A quick deal was done and after varnishing and some restoration work I sold it at auction for two hundred and fifty pounds.

There was another occasion when I had an export order for thirty typewriters to go to Africa. Unfortunately, I was stuck I had managed to get up to twenty-nine, but I was still one typewriter short. All of my business contacts were also out of machines. I was desperate for that one more. I never believe in making excuses or trying to change anything that has been agreed, so my need for that last machine was becoming urgent. Shipping was in a few days and I was stuck for that one last machine, with no idea of how I could obtain it.

The next day I needed to dispose of my waste boxes and scrap machines at the recycling depot. As I was unloading my boxes and machines at the local facility, I looked to my side and sitting there was an abandoned *Adler* manual typewriter. I thought marvellous, what a find. A quick fiver to the yardman and the machine was off to my workshop where it was to meet with its twenty-nine cousins. The full thirty machines were ready on time, all looking spic and span and were off to start a new life in Ghana.

You must not go scavenging at these disposal depots, that is definitely not on, but as you are disposing of your unwanted goods just cast an eye around where you are standing. There could be an antique typewriter sitting there waiting for a new home. The oldest typewriter in my collection is an early *Remington* of the year 1880, which was rehoused this way.

On another occasion when I was on a disposal trip, I stumbled on a small open suitcase which contained a number of old books. Some of these dated back to 1650. I pick up three which I thought worthwhile and whilst they are not valuable, I have great pleasure in reading the words written by a man about his life three hundred and fifty years ago.

SEARCHING THE INTERNET. Nowadays, the modern computer allows enthusiasts to add to their collection without walking out of the front door.

There are many buyers and sellers on the internet, there are companies which are selling at top price, and some at a give away price, either way it is an interesting place to learn from. Maybe a dealer needs to shift machines and might consider a low price offer. Remember carriage charges can be high when buying this way, especially from abroad.

ANTIQUE SHOPS. These are second-hand shops but more up-market. These shops will sell antique typewriters readily. They will usually be on the ball with values, but not always. Sometimes a quick small profit to them can be satisfying, especially if their stock holdings are high and their cash flow low.

JUMBLE SALES. Not as numerous as they were pre car-boot days, but they still exist; often in the local Church, the boy scouts huts or private clubs and so on. These outfits often have their yearly fund-raising jumble sale. Many a bargain can be had at these sales. Again, this is another place where, if you are going to be a buyer, you get there early. Many dealers pay an extra entrance fee to get in before the main crowd turns up. By doing this they get first picking.

For many years we had a couple of very good friends who were dealers, a lovely charming pair. They were elderly and were both retired, but not having a decent pension to live on, they both turned to being middle dealers. They would buy from all the places I have described and then sell whatever it might be on to an appropriate dealer or shop. We knew Greta and Jack for many years and they became a constant source of second-hand typewriters for us to buy from.

In those days I was working six full days a week and Sunday morning was the time to drive over to this couple's house and buy from them the items they might have acquired for me during the previous week.

This couple found enjoyment and wealth and kept their brains bright and alert. Jack would look out for the mechanical contraptions, such as typewriters of all kinds for me, and all sorts of clocks for another shop. Many mechanical items he would buy, repair, advertise and sell on to a new owner. Greta, however, specialised in the more delicate ladylike items, things like silver, gold, precious stones, old lace, tapestries, rare buttons, all the valuable brands of pottery and glassware, old paintings, water colours, sketches, picture frames, mechanical toys, old toys and dolls, the list could go on and on. She seemed to know enough about all these subjects to be able to buy them at the right price; and not only know where there was a source to sell them to, but also to know how much to ask for them all as well.

I have just remembered books, old books. "You never know what you might find in old books," Greta told me one day. Then she told me a tale.

"I bought some very old books for five pounds and flicking through, as I always do, a pencil portrait fell out," she said. "I thought it looked good enough to get valued." Special items that looked valuable she and her husband would take up to the London Auction Rooms for a free valuation. This little portrait turned out to be a son of a Spanish King who ruled around the year of 1550, and this was the second only portrait known to exist. She eventually sold it in auction for over four thousand pounds, this was for her a nice find.

Another Greta' buy was in an antique shop. In these places people usually know values, but not always. Browsing in one of these shops one day, she spotted an oil painting hanging on the wall, instinct alerted her to this one. She asked how much it was and the salesman replied, "To you, one hundred and twenty pounds." Geta asked him to hold it for her while she went home to get some money. She nipped home, looked through her reference books - the painter was a known name. So she took a chance, went back to the shop, did a deal for one hundred pounds, and the picture was hers. On her next trip to the London Auction Rooms, her picture went as well.

"Any good?" she asked the valuer.

"Yes, I should think it will reach nine or ten," he replied.

"Nine or ten what?" she asked.

"Nine or ten thousand pounds, of course," he snapped. (Apparently you are supposed to know they talk in thousands.)

Just a final note on this buying business: don't forget the price asked is not always the final price. Always haggle on the price go in low you can always go up if you have to.

One more tale.

A serious big time collector I know, told me recently how he went to a German Auction Room sale to bid for a rare *Hanson* ball typewriter of about 1867. He set himself a limit of twenty-five thousand pounds, but failed to buy it as it sold for thirty-seven thousand pounds. He told me that a similar typewriter had just sold in a another auction for nearly fifty thousand. This is big stuff. The most I have paid is two hundred and that was for an old and rare dictation machine, and recently, five hundred pounds for a *William's* typewriter. If you want to be a collector of old typewriters start low and learn the game. There are many machines about for as low as five to ten pounds, so good luck, and good hunting.

Apart from the existing antique collectors' market, there is a new market forming for collectors of classic typewriters (manufactured from around 1950 to 1970). The world's manufacturer's fought each other for the lion's share of this massive multi-million sales' market. All they could do to catch the purchaser's eye and wallet, was to use designs with attractive shapes and bright colours, this they did in every way they could. These machines, with their bright body colours of bold reds, blacks, whites, browns, pinks, greens, blues, yellows, even multi-coloured, are a joy to see, own and use. These Antique and Classic, machines should increase in value as time makes them less available and collectors become more.

The following pages show the world's long awaited start of "clear writing", as we see the beginning of "writing machines". Just a few from the many designs available.

Experiments with numerous typing machines had been undertaken by various inventors from the 17th century. One of the first machines that actually typed was invented by William Burt in 1830 - a replica is held in the London Science Museum. Many years passed as did many failed attempts to make a successful machine. One strange machine was the *Hanson Writing Ball*(1867) only a few were produced and one recently sold for nearly £50,000 in a German Antique Typewriter auction.

The *Remington* Typewriter Co has the honour to claim to be the first to put a typewriter into commercial production. The gunmakers E. Remington of Ilion, New York, laid down a production line to produce the typewriter invented by Christopher Latham Sholes and Carlos Glidden in 1873. Various other inventors of that time came forward with their different designs and ideas on what they thought was

The start of the clear

WRITING MACHINES

the best machine. For many decades competition drove these inventors on to either great wealth and success or bankruptcy and oblivion.

We start to understand the difficulties of the designers as we see some of these wonderful writing machines that have touched so many people's lives all around the world for the last hundred and thirty five years.

Carlos Glidden
(1834-77)

THE WORLD'S
FIRST PRODUCTION TYPEWRITER
SHOLES AND GLIDDEN
MADE IN NEW YORK USA - 1873

Christopher Latham
Sholes (1819-90)

Christopher Sholes and Carlos Glidden were partners in the worldwide race to invent an accurate and efficient writing machine. After producing many painstaking experimental models, the desperate need for more money added to their problems. Sholes urgently sought out help. It eventually came in the form of a Mr. James Densmore, he was to take a 25% share of their potential company for $650, a large sum in 1870 but coming free with the deal was Densmore's great enthusiasm which drove all around him on and on pushing failure and rejection firmly aside. The need for more money drew in another adventure seeking investor, a Mr. George Newton Yost. It was not long before Densmore and Yost bought the full rights from the inventors, Sholes and Glidden, paying them an estimated $6000. The machine was now fully owned by Densmore and Yost but still needed a company to develop and market the product. Fortune smiles on the brave, in this case the smile came from a Mr. Philo Remington the President of the Remington Gun Making Company. (The company was desperate for new ideas to manufacture following the fall in the sale of their guns). In March 1873, Densmore and Yost signed a contract with the Remington Company to manufacture 1000 machines which were to be sold using the Remington name. At long last after 100's of years and 100's of inventors, the Typewriter was about to be born.

Remington Typewriter.

The history of the REMINGTON shows a steadily rising tide of popularity and success. It is absolutely unrivalled for all the essential qualities of a first-class writing machine.

1867. First Invention of the Typewriter now known as the Remington Standard. A few machines made by hand during this and the following years.

1873. The repeated experiments of the inventors having somewhat improved upon the first crude attempts, it was brought to the Remington factory at Ilion, N. Y.

1874. After more than a year of painstaking labor on the part of many able mechanical experts the first Remington-made machines were put upon the market.

1880. Five years after, only 1,000 machines had been sold. The public were slow to realize the value of the invention.

1882. The number increased to 2,300 machines.

1885. Five thousand machines were sold this year. It grew in popular favor. In

1890 Sales had risen to 20,000 machines per annum.

1892 Finds our standing orders to our factory of 100 machines per day inadequate to meet the rapidly increasing demand.

SEND FOR ILLUSTRATED CATALOGUE.

WYCKOFF, SEAMANS & BENEDICT,

327 BROADWAY, NEW YORK.

This advertisement of 1892 shows the progress of the early years of the Writing Machine.

Philo Remington (1816–89)
manufacturer of the first commercial typewriter.

THE NEW No. 2 HAMMOND

The Standard of Excellence.

"None but itself can be its parallel."

Alignment—Perfect and permanent.
"True as the needle to the pole, or as the dial to the sun."

Impression—Invariably uniform.
"Though deep yet clear."

Touch—Soft, light, and elastic.
"With a touch that is scarcely felt or seen."

The Hammond's claim to do the **best work** is indisputable. Write for specimen and catalogue.

THE HAMMOND TYPEWRITER CO.,
407 East 62d St., - - New York.

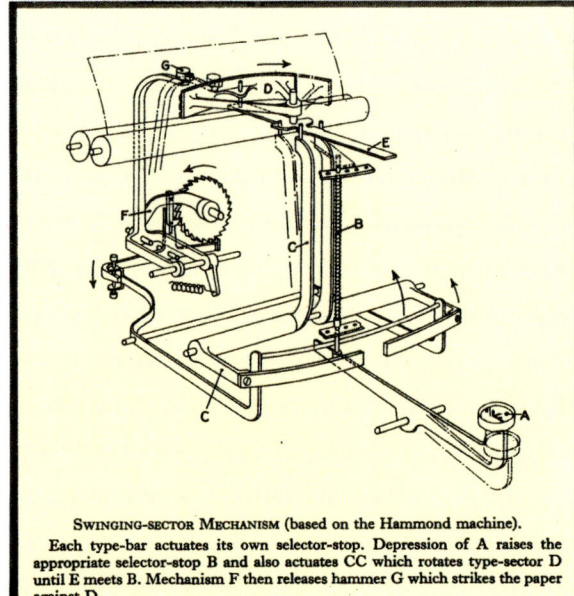

SWINGING-SECTOR MECHANISM (based on the Hammond machine).
Each type-bar actuates its own selector-stop. Depression of A raises the appropriate selector-stop B and also actuates CC which rotates type-sector D until E meets B. Mechanism F then releases hammer G which strikes the paper against D.

HAMMOND TYPEWRITER

SWINGING SECTOR MACHINE

MADE IN USA - CIRCA 1884

James Hammond had been a newspaper correspondent during the American Civil War. He was soon aware of the failing of his handwritten notes, they always seemed to change from what he had written to what was interpreted and printed. His first attempt to make a writing machine that could produce print that everyone could read, was in 1872. In 1884 the first Hammond appeared to the public - the machine has a QWERTY keyboard. The master stroke was the changeable type head known as the Swinging Sector design. The small curved sectors could come in a variety of type styles which could be easily changed and fitted. Another novel feature was holding the paper in a roll inside the wire cage.

WILLIAMS - MODEL NO:2

MADE IN CONNECTICUT USA - c 1892

Invented by John Newton Williams who spent 16 years from his first Patent in 1875 developing his remarkable "Grasshopper" machine until production commenced in 1891. Famous for its <u>Visible Writing</u>, the main feature of the Williams Writing Machines is that the type bars are in two sections, front and back of the writing line. The type heads, when in their rest position, are face down on to a re-inking pad. By pressing a key top the inked letter hops from front or back and performs a neat Grasshopper movement onto the paper. One of the main disadvantages with the machine was that the design had type heads flashing through the air from front and back which meant there was nowhere for the paper to go, well not quite nowhere, the paper had to be curled and inserted into the basket in front of the platen which as typed upon fed through to the rear basket where it could be withdrawn "Rolled Up". An outstanding machine but they could not compete against the growing competition. They fell to the Receiver in 1909 less than 20 years from their startup.

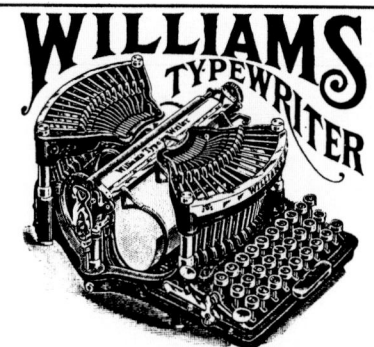
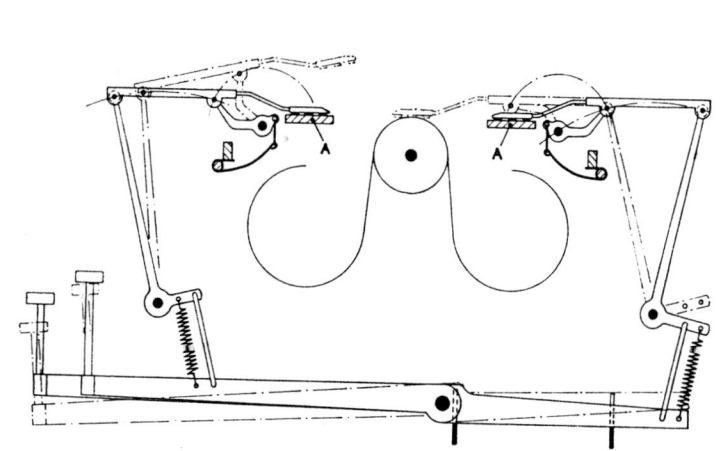

GRASSHOPPER MECHANISM (based on the Williams machine).

The type-bars are grouped in two parallel rows on each side of the platen, each group operated by half of the keys. Ink pads are shown at A.

OLIVER SIDE STRIKE OFFICE TYPEWRITER

MADE IN USA 1894

Invented by the Rev. Thomas Oliver in 1891, his patented machines began production in 1894 in the USA. The machines were well built and designed for robust service, the type action striking down on to the platen either from the left or right hand sides. The three bank keyboard and visable writing made this a successful machine. Production was moved to Croydon in England in 1928 where this style of Oliver was made until 1941. Other Oliver models followed until the Company fell to the Receiver and closed in 1971 almost 80 years after commencing.

Side Strike in Action

MIGNON ROTARY HEAD TYPEWRITER

1903 - 1933

This odd looking machine was the first Olympia typewriter that was sold as the Mignon. They were produced by AEG of Germany with production lasting for 30 years with over 350,000 of this type being made and sold.

The design was one of the Indicator Type of machine. Although odd to us now days, it was apparently liked and easy to use. Just point the pointer at the letter required and press down the control key. that would bring the rotary numbered and lettered cylinder down onto the paper. The Indicator Plate and the Type Head Cylinder could be removed and changed to other styles of print.

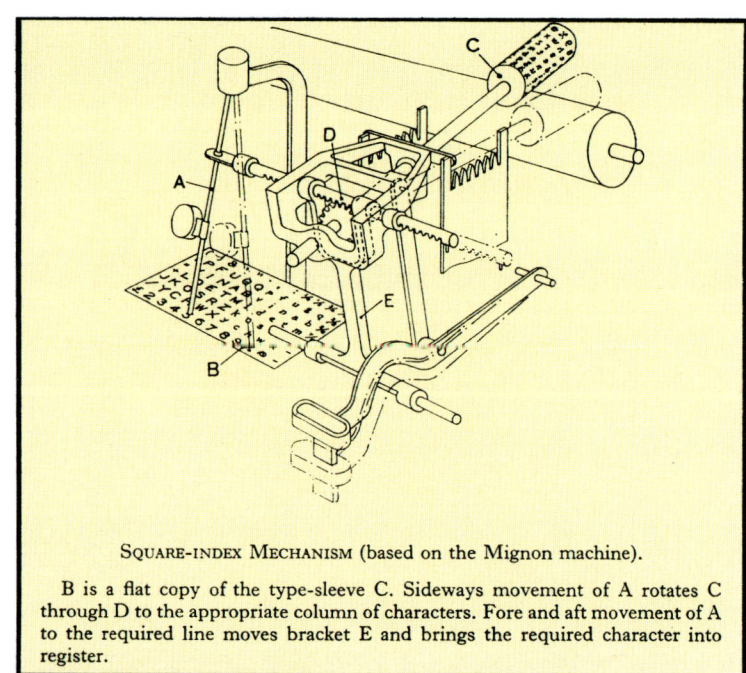

SQUARE-INDEX MECHANISM (based on the Mignon machine).

B is a flat copy of the type-sleeve C. Sideways movement of A rotates C through D to the appropriate column of characters. Fore and aft movement of A to the required line moves bracket E and brings the required character into register.

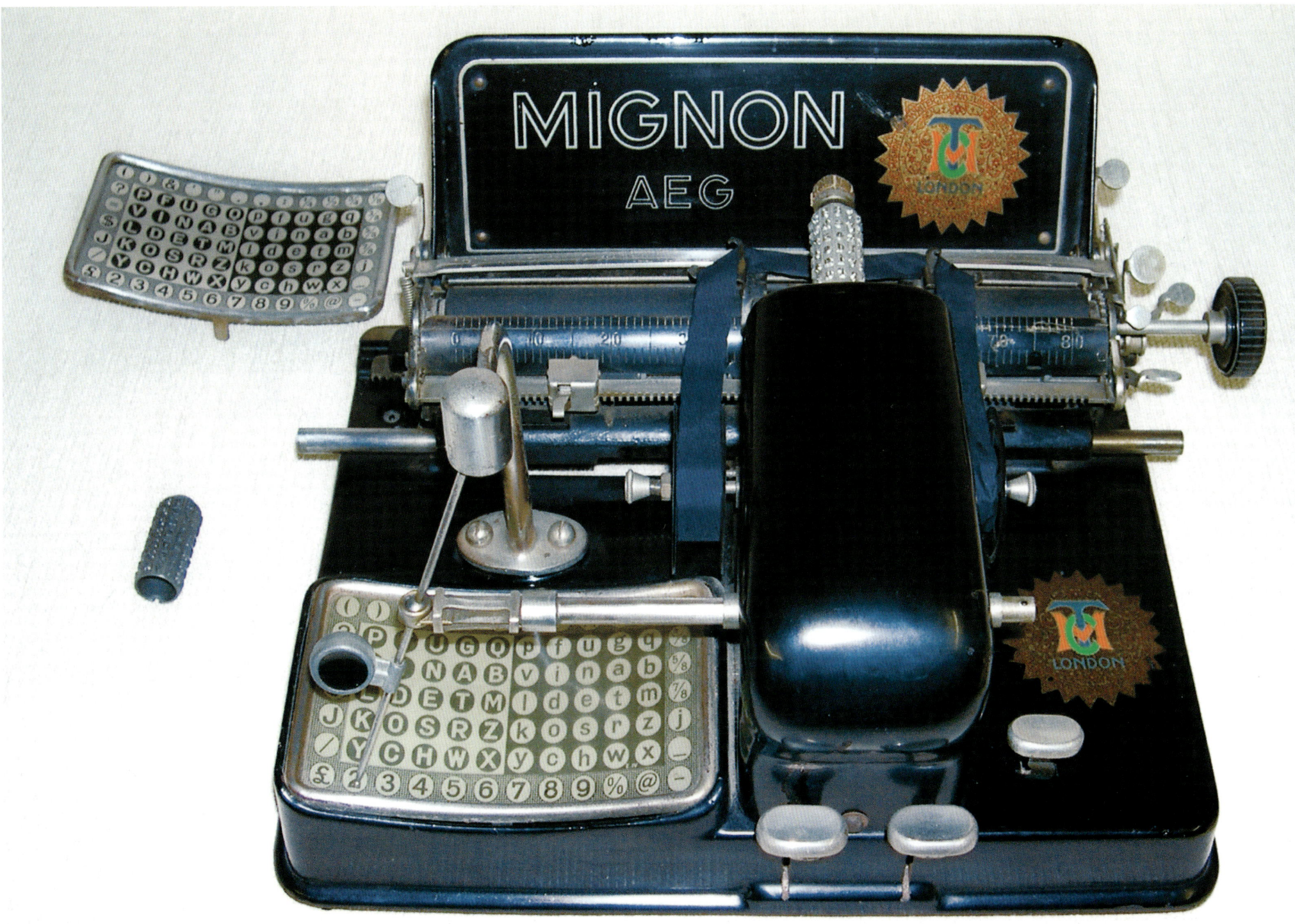

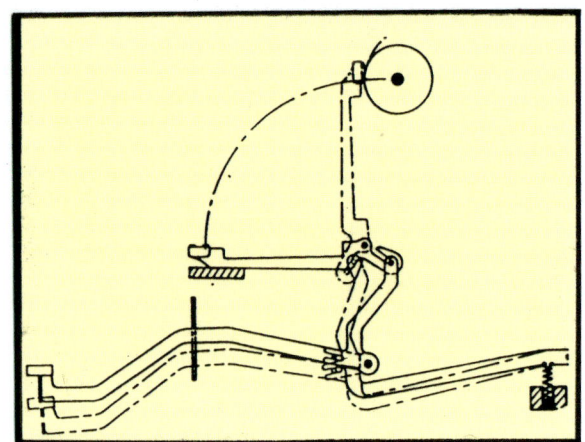

CORONA
STANDARD TYPEWRITER COMPANY

CORONA
STANDARD TYPEWRITER COMPANY

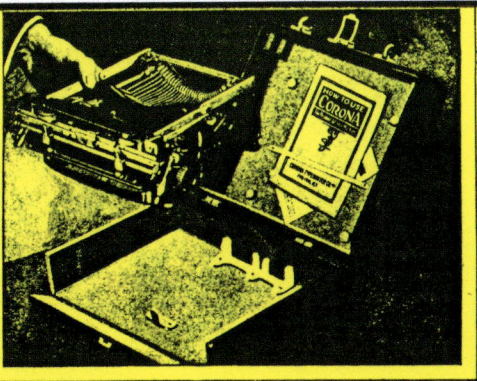

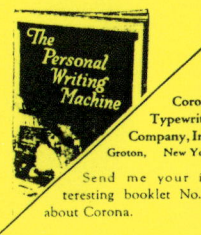

Showing the foldable Corona Typewriter in its typing position (Left) and in its stow in the case folded position (Right). Portable typewriters such as these were the tools of the roving Journalist. Lightweight portables such as the Corona were even used strapped to the knee of Journalists reporting on the spot under action in the First World War trenches.

Observer Trench

BLICKENSDERFER LIGHTWEIGHT PORTABLE

MODEL - SERVICE BLICK

MADE IN THE USA - c 1893

Invented by George C Blickensderfer of Connecticut USA in 1893. This model was one of the world's first lightweight portable laptops. A brilliant piece of engineering with its changeable print head that gave the machine the means of a wide variety of print styles. Inking was obtained by an ink pad positioned between the print head and the paper. This early model has the keyboard layout known as the Ideal Keyboard. However, the Blicks were soon to succumb to the leading keyboard design - the QWERTY. The Blick advertising cartoon seen here, makes the point about the machine's mobility. The sketch shows a Reuter's war correspondent astride a galloping camel, binoculars in one hand, the other hand on the Blick ready to record events.

Reuter's Special Correspondent, as he appeared writing despatches on the " BLICK " in the Omdurman Campaign.

"I first used a Blick in the Soudan and if I am destined to see another Campaign I shall employ 'The War Correspondent's Best Friend.'"

LIONEL JAMES,
"Times" Special Correspondent.

MACHINE VALUE

The value of Antique Typewriters varies in the same manner as all collectable items. The important considerations are:

CONDITION: Wear and tear, discoloration, loss of decal transfers and pitted plating.

WORKING OR NOT: A fully working machine is always a joy to the owner, therefore of much greater value than a non - working one.

RARITY: Many old machines are low in value, some models were made in their millions with many surviving today. However, some machines had a short production life and naturally are of higher value.

UNUSUAL DESIGNS: The more unusual the design the more interesting it becomes to most collectors and usually more valuable.

SERIAL NUMBER: The earlier the number the more valuable the machine is the general rule, but not always, and they are often a job to find.

COLOUR: Bright colours were rarely used in the earlier machines. However, in the Classic Machines dating from around 1950 or so, colour was used with great success including all shades of blue, green, white, yellow, orange, red, pink, and many others.

RESTORING: This can be a complete restoration costing a lot of money or it can be a partial restoration where anyone with a little care, can improve a machine's appearance:

A) Cleaning always helps, even those old machines that have often survived up to a century of smokers. The brown stain that a good cleaner removes, is not pleasant, however, once cleaned a drop or two of "3 in 1" oil on a cloth rubbed over the machine will bring back a shine like new.

B) Damaged paint work, small chips and scratches can be carefully touched in with paint and brush.

C) The platen i.e. roller can be cleaned with a suitable foam cleaner and a light rub with a soft pad.

D)   Re-new ribbons with red/black if the machine is designed to take them.

All this applies to the average machine which needs smartening up. If you come across a rare valuable machine it is best left to the experts to restore.

Any values given are only a guide to the prices paid in various auctions in various countries and it is to be remembered that auction values depend on competition between bidders i.e. buyers. Therefore, the more bidders the higher the final price. Few bidders or even one can result in low prices paid, sad if you are a seller but pretty good if you are the buyer. Good luck if you become a collector and good luck if you don't.